Unchained Mind

POWERFUL LIFE CHANGING THOUGHTS ON PEACE, LOVE, AND SUCCESS

RICARDO G. WILLIAMS

authorHOUSE®

AuthorHouse™
1663 Liberty Drive
Bloomington, IN 47403
www.authorhouse.com
Phone: 1 (800) 839-8640

Published by AuthorHouse   03/14/2017

ISBN: 978-1-5246-8371-9 (sc)
ISBN: 978-1-5246-8370-2 (e)

Library of Congress Control Number: 2017903938

CONTENTS

To my wife, Anjanette Williams, the love of
my life, and my family and friends.

Special thanks to my daughter, Zuri
Williams, for the gift of your life.

To my sons, Amir and Kelayda. Amir, your drive
for success is an inspiration to me. Kelayda, your
wisdom and striving for peace motivate me.

To my mom, thank you for giving me the best life.

To my brothers and sisters, Wayne, Karen,
Sandra, Toni. I love you all.

To my best friend, Jolyn Robichau, thanks
for the many years of friendship.

INTRODUCTION

I took a three-year break from work to explore the topic of peace, love, and success. During that time, I analyzed my thoughts and the effects thoughts had on my emotional state. The things I found out were intriguing. I came to realize that many of us aren't living to our full potential. We live with a measured joy. We keep our happiness in check. Our smiles are met with restriction from our breath, which makes them short-lived. We seldom breathe fully because our breathing is interrupted by the depth of our thoughts. We never let go fully. We are bound by layers of chains that have entangled our thinking: chains of an uncertain future, chains of work, chains of relationships, chains of finances, chains too many to mention.

My time away from work gave me the opportunity to explore how to break these chains. I admit that even a broken chain is not permanently broken; it can be easily be reunited if old habits are not changed. It takes awareness and action to keep broken chains broken. *Unchained Mind* focuses on the actions we can take to break chains and keep them broken.

This book explores how our thoughts control our destiny. It teaches thought control and the importance of silence. It also teaches how to overcome fear, anger, negative thoughts, stress, and hatred. You will learn how to nurture your emotions and embrace moments as well as the importance of spiritual peace. I will teach you how to live in thankfulness with compassion while activating love.

Unchained Mind will help you overcome obstacles and exercise patience while reinventing yourself. It will bring clarity to your life journey, helping you find your purpose, take risks, and avoid distractions. It will teach you how to align with the right team to fulfill your goals. The ultimate takeaway from my book is to live in freedom.

When I started writing, my initial attitude was "I will be a leader in the field of self-development and rescue others from oppressive thoughts. I will help them live in freedom embracing peace, love, and success." There are times when that vision was replaced by thoughts like *I won't amount to anything. I'm not qualified. I'm not a theologian. I am not a psychologist.* There were so many *nots* that they are too numerous to mention. I was multitasking in nots. The nots had tied a knot over my spirit. I was tied up in knots.

As I persisted in my writing, those knots began to break. Instead of multitasking with nots, I started to pursue an impossible dream of bringing my writings into a classroom where others could interpret my thoughts and share their views. People started to show their appreciation for what my thoughts had done in their lives, so I decided to compile my thoughts into books. I have moved on from fearing the impossible to living the impossible.

What are the nots in your life? Are you going to multitask with nots or are you going to embrace and live in the purpose God bestowed on you? It is my hope that *Unchained Mind* helps you loosen the nots so you can live to your full potential.

Acknowledgments

Thank you to friends who have followed my writings on Facebook, too numerous to mention, as well as to my friends Roger Downey, Uncle Martan, Evangelist Lloyd Patrice, William Workcuff, Tammie Olson, and Florence Gonzalez.

WE ARE THE PRODUCTS OF OUR THOUGHTS

Thought of the Day

Our thoughts are the seeds of life, and the thoughts we plant bear the fruits we sow.

Thoughts of fear bear fruits of fear. Thoughts of hatred bear fruits of hatred. Thoughts of love bear fruits of love. When we plant seeds of love where seeds of fear and hatred exist, we are potentially growing a beacon of hope for love to exist, even in the most barren of soils.

If we treat our thoughts the way we treat food, we digest what's good and reject what's bad. We take in enough to satisfy us and dispose of waste. When we eat a fruit, seldom do we eat the entire fruit. We eat the pulp and may discard the skin and the seed. Similarly, when we absorb our thoughts, we can differentiate among the pulp, the seed, and the skin. We can discard the thoughts that bring negativity to us and embrace thoughts that bring happiness, joy, peace, and tranquility.

If we embrace thoughts that say we're unworthy, not good enough, or have no future, we may be consuming the skin and the seeds of doubt that should be discarded and not absorbed.

There is a Buddhist quote that says, "We are what we think. All that we are arises from our thoughts. With our thoughts, we make the world." We can refocus on the thoughts that uplift us and ignore the ones that bring us down. Let's spread seeds of love in everything we do today.

Thought of the Day

Sometimes it's necessary for us to reshuffle our thoughts until we get the results we're looking for.

Our thoughts are like a deck of cards. We don't have to settle for the hand that we've been dealt. We can reshuffle our thoughts by tilting our head back and breathing in while moving it from side to side. The old thoughts will be gone, and the new thoughts will replace them.

The problem is that sometimes we become addicted to our old thoughts. Sometimes we purposefully cling to negative and damaging thoughts. We've mastered negativity in our lives so that sometimes negative thoughts are downloaded into our subconscious.

If we don't like the results of our thoughts, we can change them. This means changing the environment that we've settled into. It means seeking an alternative route. Sometimes it is necessary to stop what we're doing, look out the window, and admire life as it unfolds.

Just for today, let's promise to reshuffle our thoughts and embrace positive thoughts only.

Thought of the Day

A simple rule of thumb for stress control is never to allow our thoughts to outpace our breathing.

During stressful situations, we often get the feeling our thoughts are racing out of control. It feels like our head is spinning as our body tries to keep up with the pace of our thoughts. By focusing on calming our breathing, we can channel our thoughts and slow them down to the pace of our breathing. In doing so, we can regain control of stressful situations.

There is a constant battle between our thoughts and our breathing.

Fear restricts breathing. When we spend quiet time in our day, putting our fears at ease, we can usher in emotions of love while restoring peace in our world.

Just for today, let's promise to regulate our thoughts to a pace slower than our breathing.

Thought of the Day

The one who controls our mind controls our thinking. The one who controls our thinking controls our victory.

When we see the world through the optimistic eyes of a tourist, we experience a new outlook on life.

What's on your mind today? Is it joy, or is it sadness? Is it peace, or is it despair? Many of us have lived with painful thoughts for a long time, so we've built a brick wall of pain around our soul. The pain of the thoughts feels like it is stuck in our heart.

Remember how it was when you saw a new place for the first time? Remember the feeling of inserting a plastic key in a hotel door and walking into a tidy, nice-smelling room? You can recreate that feeling with each day. You can examine your thoughts. You can change your outlook and view each moment through the optimistic eyes of a tourist. If you do, you may welcome a new wave of awe and excitement.

Thought of the Day

When we free congesting thoughts from our minds, we welcome peace in our soul.

The best state to experience the beauty of life in is a mindless, thoughtless state free of any emotion other than gratitude for the present moment. This is experienced only for a moment, but it is a moment worth clinging to.

We tend to attach to our emotional state of being, and our thoughts can create detours in our lives. We fluctuate among anger, anxiety, fear, sorrow, and disgust. When we control our thoughts, we control our experiences. We can turn bad situations into good ones.

Take a deep breath and then focus on your breathing, not on your thoughts. If you do, you may free your mind, calm your emotions, and open the door to peaceful moments.

Thought of the Day

If we know it's wrong, then why do we entertain it?

Our faith walk with God is a parallel one, and many forces we come up against can pull us away from our walk. These forces attack us where we are most vulnerable, in our places of need. When we succumb to them, as the momentary satisfaction disappears, so does our spirituality.

When our parallel walk with God is broken, the only way to restore it is to spend time in the presence of the great Physician. We should pray hard and pray intensely for our restoration because the path of brokenness leads to death.

In our solitary moments, we can start the restoration of our soul. It may take time, but if we make the time, we may regain our spiritual strength and experience a feeling of being renewed and reenergized.

When we pursue the thoughts we know are wrong, we feed our mind with contaminated thoughts. Every potentially bad moment starts with a thought, so if we know it's wrong, we should not entertain it. When bad thoughts enter our mind, we can hit the delete button and welcome good thoughts instead.

Thought of the Day

Sometimes the best opinion to have is none.

Opinions spark discussions, and sometimes we're so busy sticking to our own opinions that we barely hear the opinions of others. Sometimes we go back and forth, shouting our opinions over each other. In the end, we walk away frustrated and depressed that no one embraced our opinions.

The time we spend defending our opinions can be put to better use, especially if we choose not to have the opinions at all. We could use that time to create an environment of peace within us by spending quiet time alone.

In life, we must choose our battles. Sometimes it's necessary to let things go untampered with. Sometimes it's necessary to have no opinions. We can take a moment to clear our mind of all opinions and get a fresh outlook on life.

Thought of the Day

Deep in the absence of thought, a bed of heavenly peace awaits us.

We possess the ability to welcome and discard thoughts that may dwell within us and create either harmony or disharmony. We should always be mindful of that power and use it.

What if we discovered within us a replica of the Garden of Eden? What if we discovered there are certain fruits in the garden that we should not eat? What if eating those fruits disrupts the peace of our garden and confine us to feelings of guilt?

Think about it this way: if love, kindness, compassion, peace, and joy are the fruits of your garden, there is a good chance you are experiencing the heavenly state of being. However, if hate, gossip, fear, and greed are the fruits of your garden, you may be banishing yourself to a hellish state of existence.

We can spend time in stillness to acquire a state of mind of thoughtlessness, where the only thing that matters is the heavenly peace that awaits us.

2

REMOVING TOXIC
EMOTIONS FROM
WITHIN

Thought of the Day

We will not truly regain our peace until we give our peace to silence.

In this fast-paced world of information given to us by the media, our peace is swept away in turmoil. Anxiety is up; fear is up; chaos is up. Our state of mind and health go up in flames in the turmoil.

However, we can regain our peace by temporarily shutting down our media intake and engaging in total silence. We can focus on the sound of the waves of our breathing as they wash up against the shores of our nostrils. We can focus on the waves of our breathing as they sweep away thoughts in their path.

It may take an hour, or it may be longer, but we can take whatever amount of time is necessary to restore our sanity. At some point, the sound of our breath in waves will go away, and all that will be left is the dead of silence. In that moment, we will be totally restored.

The first moments of the mornings are the best time to engage in moments of solitude.

Thought of the Day

When we have fear in our hearts, the fear we face has already won.

What are you afraid of? Is it on its way, or is it already knocking at our door? Is it already here? Have you secured a room in your heart to accommodate fear? Is it growing deeper every day?

Today is the day to replace fear with joy, peace, and love in our hearts. We can be bold as we walk through the valley of fear, for somewhere along the path of fear victory is waiting for us. We can use the gifts of our lives, which God has bestowed on us, to live a life free from fear.

We can take a deep breath, smile, and welcome joy, love, and peace back.

Thought of the Day

Our neglected emotions become hiding grounds for the things that can harm us.

I always look for a deeper meaning in my experiences. Recently, I killed a snake, and it didn't even have teeth. It was hiding under my abandoned kitchen garden, under the overgrown weeds and grass. It found warmth in the mess I had created. It found warmth where I had created neglect.

This got me thinking. *What are the snakes in my life? What are the neglected areas that are giving warmth to my snakes? Am I giving teeth to my snakes?*

I decided to do a major cleanup of my neglected emotions, and I uncovered hidden snakes that gave warmth to my fears. Now the fears are diminished, and so are the snakes.

What are the things that keep your snakes warm? What is disrupting your peace of mind? Are you cleaning up the areas in your life that have been left abandoned because of the mess you've made?

Spend some time today cleaning up negative emotions and welcoming new beginnings.

Thought of the Day

It is necessary to remove yesterday's thoughts that have transformed into painful emotions before adding today's thoughts.

Jesus called this adding new wine to old wineskin. Some of us are bursting right now with high blood pressure, heart conditions, and stress. We battle painful emotions, while we hold on to painful past experiences. However, we don't have to live with the emotional pain.

You can sit quietly, focus on the pain inside, and push it out of you. Breathe out with the pain, and when it's gone, welcome the positive thoughts of the new day. You may need to the repeat the cycle as many times as you need to master it.

The waste products of life—be they food, air, or water—become toxic after they serve their purpose. We should spend some time to expel yesterday's emotional pain from today's reality. The trauma of yesterday is over. We shouldn't search our minds to bring it back from the dead. It's a new day. There will be new beginnings. There will be new things to look forward to. There will be new ventures to be excited about.

Bring love, compassion, and kindness into the new day. Trust your instincts even as you serve others. Let them be your guide as you create harmony into your life.

Let's play our part in recreating the perfect world. Remember, we can be part of the solution or part of the problem, but the goal is to make the world a better place because of our presence, and we should have fun doing it.

Thought of the Day

Anger can be a catalyst that propels inner rage to collide with outward rage. When it does, it doubles the catastrophe.

We all have reasons to be angry. Unforeseen bills, the rising cost of living, health care expenses, labels—the list can go on and on. Every day it seems that we adjust to accommodate one more piece of news that adds to our reason to feel angry. It gets worse even when things seem to get better.

We may want to throw a permanent pity party, but what good will it do in this temporary journey we call life? Is it wise to spend our last days feeling sorry for our condition in the world, or is it better to spend it seeing what is left of its beauty? We shouldn't be pessimistic about our circumstances. We can be eternally optimistic. Pessimism breeds pessimism, and optimism breeds optimism.

We've made it this far. We've crossed many intimidating rivers and grown from strength to strength in the process. We can take ownership of anger. We can laugh at ourselves instead of entertaining anger. With humility, we can forgive ourselves. We can resist the temptation to blame others. We can pray in silence for the forgiveness of our soul, and we can move on in optimism, growing stronger and stronger each moment.

Thought of the Day

We should not speak negative thoughts, whether they are toward ourselves, our friends, or our enemies. In the end, negativity is stored within us, and it disrupts our peace of mind.

Social media is good for connecting with family, friends, and our world. However, it's also a breeding ground for negativity. Whether we're talking about negativity about the news media, politics, religion, or oppression, social media feeds us with all the negativity we can digest and more. When we feel overwhelmed, it's good to analyze the toxic information we've been gathering within us.

Before you start your day, spend time in solitude to remove the negativity of yesterday from within you, before you indulge in the negativity of today.

Thought of the Day

Our emotional toxic waste emerges from the source that feeds it. The source that is strongest manifests its waste the most.

We normally dispose of waste before it becomes toxic. We discard digested food waste carefully and privately. So why do we treat our toxic emotional waste differently? Why do we assume that others will be okay with our abuse, anger, hatred, frustrations, whining, and complaining?

We neglect to cleanse our emotions daily. Why? Because we're holding on to fear, bitterness, failure, and self-doubt? Because we're not spending quiet times in mindless meditations? Because we're getting the wrong spiritual nourishment? Whatever the reason, it's important to attend to our toxic emotions and to discard them in a safe and secure manner before they become harmful.

Just for today, we can attend to our emotional needs. We can clasp our hands, extend them above our head, then stretch and breathe deeply.

Thought of the Day

It is better to live free and die free than to spend a lifetime chained in agony.

We sometimes treat our hearts like storage beds for our emotional experiences. We tend to hold on to the things we feel passionate about. Though sleep is a perfect avenue to start anew, our subconscious mind sometimes remains infected by the negative emotions we don't let go. We become crippled by the emotions we hold on to. But it doesn't have to be that way. We don't have to hold on to emotions that will eventually lead to our own demise.

In our waking moments, we can examine our hearts. We can weed out negativity and breathe it out of our being. When we do this, we may regain our spiritual peace of mind, and we may experience a special kind of joy to our lives.

Let's live free and die free.

Thought of the Day

We should never turn a burning house into a fireplace to warm and comfort us.

The most damaging thing to the foundation of peace is negative emotions. Many of us are aware of their presence, but we do nothing to expunge them. Instead we warm ourselves in their uncomfortable presence, allowing them to control us instead of putting them to good use.

Singers put their emotions into their performances; the inflections of their voices are synchronized with body movements that enhance the emotional expression. We may not be great singers, but we have what it takes to connect with the pain of our deeply embedded emotions and bring them to the forefront. However, most of us don't, and we suffer the consequences as we harvest negative emotions. We harvest hurt instead of confronting pain. We protect our hurt and lash out at anything that feels like it's going to unearth our pain.

Negative emotions, including from past hurts, don't need a body to keep them sheltered. They need an outlet so they can be expressed and released from within.

Some of the greatest and most successful people turn their negative, painful emotions into expressive art. But those of us who aren't artists don't have to live with the pain either; we can express it in our own songs, dances, and acts.

When we spend time alone, flushing out unwanted emotions, we can experience peace. But peace is not a constant; it requires constant work, moment by moment.

Thought of the Day

We can spend time putting out the fire within us before we attempt to put out the flames on the outside.

An African proverb says, "When there is no enemy within, the enemy outside cannot hurt you."

The war we fight is the war within us, and our emotional state of mind fuels it. We can spend quiet time in silence to reset our emotions. We can take as long as necessary to put out the fire within us. We can then change the environment outside us by pouring love where there is hate. We can bring clarity where there is confusion and distortion. We can shed light where there is darkness. We can bring hope where there is despair and peace where there is war. We can then attend to the war within all over again.

Just for today, let's spend time calming the raging fires of emotions within us before we attempt to put out the flames on the outside.

Thought of the Day

When the ride of life feels bumpy, don't lose faith. Hold on and pray.

One of the challenges we face is how to get along with all our different sides—that is, the good, the bad, and the ugly. This is a personal challenge and a beautiful adventure. It's okay to apologize to others when the ride seems unbearably bumpy. The bumps and bruise are all part of the learning experience.

Sometimes it's necessary to get down on our elbows, knees, and hands, put our faith in the presence of God, and allow him to calm the storms of emotions on the inside, so that we are in a better positioned to calm the storms on the outside.

Thought of the Day

When we knowingly house a destructive guest, we're just as responsible for the damage done.

One misconception is that we can protect ourselves from the wounds of the past by shielding ourselves from anyone who exposes those wounds. Sometimes we worsen the wounds by doing irrational things that get our mind off the pain. We get involve in things like uncommitted relationships. We shop excessively for items we don't need or can't afford. We do such things to escape the pain of the wounds inside us. The pain may go away temporarily, but the damage is sometimes long-term.

To attend to wounded emotions, we need to be aware of their presence. We are the CEOs of our decisions. We are the presidents of our experiences. And we are the governments of our dependencies. With those credentials in mind, we can take control of all areas of our lives and project a successful, brighter future while taking the steps necessary to get there. We can cut out wasteful spending. We can save and create a surplus for our future. We can invest in our goals, our dreams, and our careers. We can attend to our health and our emotions. We can defend ourselves against the things that affect our peace, and we can live by faith that God has given us the tools to be great.

Pray on it. Cry on it. Groan on it. Comfort it. Forgive it. Then push it out. Release it from within you, so that you won't have to deal with it repeatedly. If it shows up again, follow the same principles, repeating the process until it goes away permanently.

Before we enter into a panic mode, we can say a quick thank-you to God. If that doesn't work, we can say it like we mean it. If that doesn't work, we can embrace it in a happy dance or a happy song.

Sometimes as I relax in my bathtub, listening to music with my headphones on, I pretend for a moment that I'm blind. As I feel myself entering into a panic over the possibility that this temporary blindness will be permanent, I say a quick thank-you for my sight. If that doesn't work, I embrace the song I'm listening to and sing it from the depths of my soul. If that doesn't work, I try the process over again. We rarely conquer things the first time. Sometimes we have to start over.

If in your efforts to succeed you don't go deeper than you did before, you may find yourself spinning in circles and getting the same results. Take some time to reassess your process. Come up with new ways to make peace with your fears by confronting them in a safe environment. Take a deep breath, and start over again.

Thought of the Day

No matter how many good days we have, they don't prepare us for the bad days that may come.

When bad days come, we shouldn't despair. We can dig deep into our trenches and wait it out. We can regroup and rise. We can avoid self-condemnation, for it is self-destructive when we're at low points in life. We can be patient with ourselves, even when we make mistakes.

We should never take a sinful path lightly; instead, we can pray deeply and intensely for the restoration of our soul. We can submit our thoughts to the healing power of prayer.

We can be thankful and openly optimistic in the bad days and know that this too shall pass. The sun will be out in its glory tomorrow, and we will be out in our glory also.

Thought of the Day

When life feels like an emotional roller-coaster ride, you can hold on tight and give it all you've got. Don't forget to scream and pray.

Call me a chicken, but I'm really scared of roller-coaster rides. But I'm man enough to know that being on a roller-coaster ride with my family is more masculine than standing on the ground, watching them go through the thrill of the ride without me.

Many times in my quiet times, I revisit my roller-coaster moments. Systematically, I analyze how I handled the difficulties of not being in control of my destiny. I closed my eyes; I screamed in anticipation of the wild moments; then I held on tight with all my might. When I thought I was holding on tight enough, I wasn't, so I applied more strength and cried out to God.

I imagined that each dip and each bump was the last. I imagined that each bend and each turn was the last. I thanked God that it was over before it was over. And when it was over, I vowed I'd never get back on.

When life presents us with roller-coaster moments, how do we handle it? Do we put ourselves back in the same situation, or do we vow never to return?

Life situations present many roller-coaster experiences. Bad relationship patterns, addictions, anger, fears are all like those roller-coaster rides. They challenge our peace of mind.

We have the power to decide if we're going to get on the ride, stay on the ride, or set our standards for the kind of ride we want to experience. We should keep our faith strong and guard ourselves from the things that challenge our peace of mind.

Thought of the Day

Focus on bringing peace into your own life before attempting to bring it to others.

Our environment provides insight into our peace. When we look around, what do we see? Is it congested, or is everything nicely spaced? Congestion could be a sign of emotional congestion in our lives.

Look around. How is your spouse? How are your children? Are they in good spirits, or are they agitated? Their agitation could be an indication of agitations in your own life.

How are your pets? Are they happy, or are they scared? Ever seen a dog smile? A dog's smile is an authentic measure of peace, but it takes work to get a dog to smile. We first have to bring our smile, our peace, our love, and our affection to our dogs before we can induce them to smile.

The things around us reflect our being. If we can fix our emotional state, we are better able to clean up our environment and bring peace.

Thought of the Day

If we resolve our issues on the inside, there won't be any issues on the outside left for us to resolve.

There's something scary about facing what's inside us. We tend to focus on what's on the outside to avoid looking within. When we face situations where there is nothing left to do on the outside, we find ourselves staring through the window within. We face the eyes looking into our soul.

This can be one of the most intimidating sights we ever encounter. To some it feels like being a deer in the headlights. In those moments, thoughts of being worthless or even of suicide may pop into our mind. Having nothing to do leaves us vulnerable. We're not trained to have that kind of freedom and luxury.

When you find yourself fleeing when you have nothing to do, it is good to take a deep breath and refocus on the goals you want to accomplish and start to work on them right away.

To quote Buddha, "Endurance is one of the most difficult disciplines, but it is to the one who endures that the final victory comes." Breathe deeply. Smile frequently. Remember that there is real strength in your ability to endure all things— good and bad—with a smile and peace of mind.

Thought of the Day

Before we focus on the anger on the outside, we can first heal the anger on our inside.

We can start by accepting responsibility for our anger, not on whose fault something is. Many times, our anger comes to the surface because of a perceived injustice, whether we are right or wrong. Our fear brings out the anger in us that we label as self-defense and sometimes justice. We end up handling our anger in ways that cause us lasting damage, no matter how noble our intentions were.

But all is not lost. We can be patient with our anger and the consequences caused by our anger. Pay attention to the actions you took after your anger died, and focus on the journey that led to peace.

Did you connect with others? Did you uplift others? Did you help others understand their own anger and how to deal with it? Did anger turn you into a teacher, or did you remain housed by your anger, waiting to erupt like an uncontrollable volcano?

We can be patient with our anger. We can pay close attention to where it's leading us. We can accept responsibility for our anger, even though what caused it may not be entirely our fault. The fact that it is our anger makes us responsible. Then we can lead others to understanding how to deal with their own anger.

In the end, anger is a fight within us caused by our response to feelings of insecurity and fear. During it all, it points us to our strengths when self-doubt and inaction leave us feeling helpless and abandoned. We can use our anger to help those trapped in their own prison of anger. And the world will be a better place because of our actions.

Thought of the Day

Sometimes tears are the only form of therapy needed to heal the soul.

Can you recall the last time you cried in silence? Did you feel worse than you felt before the tears or after? We live in a society where tears are mocked and viewed as a weakness, not a strength.

Do you remember the last time you had heartfelt tears—the kind that don't fall but push your emotional pain out of the congested areas of your heart and out of your being?

Every day we feed our emotions with both positive and negative communication. The residuals build up our stress level. We can cleanse some of our stress by spending time in heartfelt tears while pushing away painful emotions. Feeling down? Make time today to shed a tear.

3

OUR CIRCUMSTANCES ARE VICTIMS OF OURSELVES

Thought of the Day

We're never victims of our circumstances. Our circumstances are victims of us. We create the circumstances we want in our lives.

Ben Franklin said, "Joy doesn't exist in the world, it exists in us."

Sometimes life's disappointments hold us captive to our past, and we feel helpless and unable to move on. It's even worse when it happens due to no fault of our own.

I remember acing an interview and was looking forward to starting a new job. But I was informed that a background check revealed some things that made me unemployable. I contacted the background check company about the inaccuracies, and they said they had made the corrections. Unfortunately the company still refused to hire me. Traumatized, I wondered how many more inaccuracies would show up, and I was afraid to apply for future jobs.

Writing was always my passion, and there I was, able to give it full-time attention. So I started writing. I changed from being a victim of my circumstances and created the circumstances I wanted. And I became a published author.

When we find ourselves stuck over bad news and unable to move on, the best thing to do is to explore our options and get busy on the things we love doing that are part of our goals—and bring them to reality.

Thought of the Day

Many may try to steal your joy, but only you can give it away freely.

I learned a very important lesson when I was a travel agent long ago. A client of mine, a Japanese ambassador, gave me a beautiful pen as a token of appreciation for taking care of his travel plans. I used the pen at my place of work, until a client who didn't have a pen borrowed it to sign a document. I never saw the pen again.

When the Japanese ambassador stopped by my office, I told him about my mishap. I foolishly asked if there was a warranty on the pen, hoping he would offer me another.

I learned that sometimes we spend our lives letting other people steal our joy, and when we get to old age, we scramble to make the best of what's left. We let people tell us what we can and can't do. We live to please others as opposed to pleasing ourselves. We should know that if night mysteriously turned to day, the people that told us the things we can't and shouldn't do might be the ones caught doing those same things.

God has given you one life. This is it. Live. Be mindful and respectful of others, but live.

Thought of the Day

When the road of life is tedious, take time out to reassess the journey.

When it feels like we're always on the run, and fatigue sets in, we should find time to sit quietly and in silence to receive all the blessings that God has in store for us.

Can we make it rain, or does rain come in due course? Can we direct the wind? Do we panic when the elements that enrich our lives are delayed?

While we're waiting, we can open our hearts to silence. While we're waiting, we can look forward to receiving the gifts that are on the horizon and moving toward us. While we're waiting, we can reassure our emotions that great things are coming our way. We can be calm, grateful, and loved. While we're waiting, we can be aware of our breath and breathe deeply.

If it feels like the road of life is rocky, and you can't find the time to reassess your journey, sit for a moment in silence. In silence, may your trust be in God, and may the depth of your breath and the strength of your groans heal the wounds of your hearts. May you be restored to the fullness of radiant living.

Thought of the Day

In the presence of God, all we need is an open heart and a clear mind ready to receive the gifts of the spirit. We need a heart free from buts, ifs, maybes, and should haves.

Many of us show up in the presence of God with our hearts tightly sealed and choked with regret and guilt. We say, "But I've sinned. If only I were more righteous. Maybe someone else is more worthy. I should not have engaged in such behavior." With guilt and condemnation, we deny ourselves the full reward of being in God's presence, and we walk away feeling no different from how we felt when we entered.

Have you ever sat in a church for an hour and walked out feeling more depressed than when you walked in? Maybe you blamed the pastor for the lack of sermon content or the congregation for worshipping too loud?

Whether we are in a crowded room or a quiet closet, if our hearts are sealed with buts, ifs, maybes, and should haves, we risk missing out on the full rewards of life. And in the end, we have only ourselves to blame. Why? Because God is always here waiting for us to step into his presence.

Thought of the Day

The presence of God is experienced in every breath we take, and we decide how we experience his presence.

How is your breathing today? Is it fearful? Is it worrisome? Is it congested? Is it full of energy? Is it filled with gratitude? Is it filled with thankfulness? Is it carrying regret, disappointment, or grief? Is it even there? Have you acknowledged its presence? If you know that the presence of God is reassuringly and abundantly available to you in whatever way you choose to experience it, will you waste it on anger? Will you waste it on hate? Or will you create an environment of peace, joy, and love?

What kind of life do you want for yourself? Only when you know the answers can you shape your life experiences and thereby experience the presence of God to the fullest.

Thought of the Day

The most complicated journey we'll take is the journey of understanding ourselves. And it's the most important.

We'll discover what makes us smile and what makes us cry. We'll discover joy, and we'll discover despair. We'll discover selfishness, and we'll discover compassion. We'll discover love, and we'll discover stubbornness. We'll discover humility, and we'll discover arrogance. We'll discover kindness, and we'll discover hatred. In all that we discover, some we will choose to live in and some we will choose to move on from. Each choice will affect our journey. Choose wisely.

Our life experiences are like a remote control that God has placed in our hands. We may lose control of it, but faith restores it. So what is controlling your remote? Is it your finances? Is it your insecurities? Is it politics or the media? Is it gossip? Or is it love? You get to flip the channel, and you choose the channel you want.

If your current situation needs change, flip the channel. You can flip the channel as many times as is needed until you find harmony.

Mohandas K. Gandhi said, "Always aim at complete harmony of thought and word and deed. Always aim at purifying your thoughts, and everything will be well."

Thought of the Day

If we give up what works, we may end up with what doesn't work. If we give up on our faith, we may end up with no hope.

We can be strong in our faith and renew it daily. If it isn't broken, there's no need to exchange it for something different. Just renew it. The grass always seems greener on the other side.

When people try to change my belief, I always tell them that I believe because it works for me. I've been tested, and it always works for me, so I'll never give up on what works and end up with something that doesn't work.

We have our religion, and we know what it says we should do and not do. But when it comes down to crunch time, true religion is the sum of a person's morals, and each person's morals are different from the other person's morals. And our moral values change the more we learn. In the end, each of us faces our own judgment and the consequences for our actions. We can avoid falling victims to things that go against our values. And we can be tolerant of others.

The challenge we face is how to make life work for the good in each of us and for others while creating harmony for all in the process. The answer may be one person at a time solving one problem at a time.

Thought of the Day

The greatest gift we have is our story.

Our life, with all its bumps and bruises along the way, will always be the greatest story ever told, if told in a way that others can experience it.

To tell our story, the important thing is getting the dialogue right. If we can relate our life stories to the dialogue that transpired during the most important events of our lives, we can capture our audience and take them on a walk through the scenic memories of our mind. In doing so, we take them on walks through parks, waterfalls, across rainbows, and among shooting stars.

Every one of us has a story. Some have silenced their story, but those who find a way to share their stories sometimes rack up bestsellers. You can start telling your story by mapping the important events in your life in short sentences. Place the events in chronological order. Create dialogue for each event from start to finish. Then let your life story unfold.

Even with the bumps and bruises of life, we all have stories that are unique and special.

Thought of the Day

When we abandon our past, we abandon the roots of our lives. And without roots, a tree is lifeless.

We should know the roots of our faith and embrace it as we travel through life. Our roots keep us grounded. We can lie on the ground and experience our grounded nature. Remember, wisdom is stored in the root of all things. It's the point of life's mistakes and lessons. We can focus on the lesson and not the mistakes. Anthony Robbins said, "Focus on where you want to go, not on what you fear."

Life is a journey of many missteps, but every step gives you a chance to correct the previous ones. Be grounded and focused. The very essence of your life is fueled by the past. I can't imagine us as Christians not being fueled by stories of the past Jesus even as we celebrate the present Jesus.

When my daughter asks me to tell her stories before she goes to bed, all my stories are about my upbringing. Surely some bad things happened in my past, but the fact that I'm alive means the bad things turned out to be great memories. And surely, I suffered losses in the past, but when I tell stories of Grandma and Grandpa, those are a forever treasure that fuels the roots of my past and that is celebrated in the present. Because of our past, we are who we are in the present.

When we celebrate our past, we open the floodgates of joy that fuel our present moments.

Thought of the Day

We can't avoid the waves when we're standing in the ocean.

Stress is the most complicated aspect of our lives, and because of its repetitive nature, it can become less complicated. We've been stressed so many times we can stand on the shores as the waves of stress flow in and command them to stop or command them to change course. We can command our thoughts to transform into happy thoughts.

But many of us try to anticipate stress rather than understand how it works. In my experience, the strongest emotions of stress occur when my mind leaves the present moment and lingers on events in the near future. An upcoming trip, the starting of a new job, the news of a possible job termination, and an unsure moment in a relationship can all trigger a rush of stressful emotions.

Stress is repetitive in nature, so a simple event, anticipating a bad day, or just knowing it's Monday can trigger stress.

Many of us wake up in a bad mood every day. We live in anticipation of stress long after the initial cause of stress is gone. It seems that the purpose of stress is to hand over our anticipations to an imaginary self.

Stress is nothing more than us standing on the shores with our mind, battling the oceans. We can control and minimize stress by focusing only on things in our present moments. We can focus on the things in our present location and design beautiful thoughts of them. We can have fun with our breathing, do some form of exercise, take a walk outside, or practice meditation. All of these reel our mind out of the depths of the ocean and secure it in our present moment.

The next time you feel the pain of stress, stop, take a moment, and ask yourself, "Where are my present thoughts located?" If they're lingering in the future, bring them back to the present, and smile. You'll soon realize that controlling your thoughts can be a fun game, not an unproductive pain.

Thought of the Day

Our shortcomings may seem like red flags of failure, but they are green lights for growth.

Recently I saw a woman with no face; her face had been eroded. I didn't know how to respond to what I saw: a scared, self-conscious woman moving through life like a deer in the headlights, wondering who would be the next person to judge her?

I failed to realize that I was looking at myself and my own shortcomings. I was judging her based on my standards.

When was the last time you were afraid of someone because of his or her skin color, religious belief, or sexual orientation? When was last time you feared someone because of that person's economic status? Each person's life is a reflection of our own life. We can bring joy to anyone we encounter if our joy is like a glowing candle of love within us.

Thought of the Day

We pass or fail every test we experience based on the level of success we give to it.

We can embrace peaceful transformations in all our moments. Have you ever imagined being locked in the trunk of a moving car? I didn't until I saw it depicted on a TV show. What would you do in such a situation? Would you find peace? Or would you be terrified in that small confined area?

However we perceive our situation determines the outcome. In the end, we are either stronger because of it or weaker. And most situations will not be that taxing.

We can stop, take a deep breath, and calm ourselves. Whatever we're going through today, we can embrace peaceful moments, and peace will be the level of our success.

Thought of the Day

We can experience heaven or hell, depending on how we embrace our past. And faith will hand us God's kingdom.

Can we experience heaven? What if we could retract our footprints and make each step better than it was before?

Can we experience hell? What if we retrace our footprints and make each step worse than it was before?

Can we experience the kingdom of God? What if we retract our footprints and let God stamp a seal of approval on each step?

We often try to be perfect in the eyes of others, imprisoning our real self. We imprison our emotions. We store up scared emotions, hurt emotions, subdued emotions. We sometimes smile when we're hurting. Life has taught us that failure is the worst thing we can ever face. Life has taught us that we must not disappoint others by making fools of ourselves, so we do things to make others happy at the expense of ourselves.

What if we found out that people are so busy trying to subdue their prisoners that they have no time to look at the chaos outside of their prisons? Yes, they may make a comment or two, but that doesn't mean we're forever on their mind?

If at a choir performance you haven't sang a song from the depths of your soul, ruined the performance, and possibly banned from ever returning, you might be living with imprisoned emotions. If you haven't danced in a carnival or street festival and the next day felt you had to wear a hat and sunglasses, you might be living with imprisoned emotions. If you haven't shouted from the depth of your heart, there's a chance you're living with imprisoned emotions. Now may be a good time to free your emotions and not be held hostage by pretense. It's important that our expressions of joy free us from our deepest imprisoned emotions.

Thought of the Day

Guilt is an unreasonable burden to carry.

There are no bad treasures in our past, yet everything we experienced was meant to teach us something. When I look back at my past, I find myself smiling at the things I thought were bad. The things that were really bad, I seem to have no recollection of.

I can now write about the bad things and profit from those experiences. There was a time I felt trapped in my bad experiences, but now I feel I have what it takes to let go of the past. I embrace the sense of power that gives me.

If I had an opportunity to do my past over, I wouldn't change a thing. I'd experience it just the way life presented it to me. I'd handle it with my limited understanding, just the way I handled it as a child. No more guilt, no more sorrow—just God's blessings.

I'm not always right, and yesterday I was wrong, so forgive me, and let's move on.

So many times we're stuck in a moment of stubbornness because we didn't get our way with things. And we miss the beauty of the moment. Worse yet, when life reveals that we are wrong, we feel we're too big to say we are wrong or too big to apologize. To amend the past, it's important that we acknowledge our mistakes so that future generations, which stems from the past, know that we've moved on and made amends.

When we fail to acknowledge our wrongdoings, and we move on with a convicted spirit, we inflict wounds on our soul. When we feel convicted, we should stop, take a moment of silence, drop any pressing matters, and clear every thought. We need to attend to our emotions and to stretch and breathe deeply until the pain of conviction goes away.

Thought of the Day

When we know the seasons of our lives, we can make full use of the harvest.

If we don't know it's spring, we miss the refreshing morning breeze that ushers in the most beautiful days of the year. We may missed that day if we approach it with a winter state of mind. Such is the importance of awareness. We wouldn't prepare for snow in the spring. We wouldn't walk out our doors in the early mornings with a shovel. Instead, we would put on our jogging pants or take the dogs for a walk.

How are we treating the seasons of our lives? Are we living in winter when spring is all around us? Are we so busy worrying about everything that isn't present that we are missing the blessings presented to us?

Just for today, embrace the seasons. Bring out the spring! Walk with an extra spring in your step. Embrace your confidence. Breathe in the freshness of the new day, and rejoice in the opportunities.

Thought of the Day

Even a warrior needs a place of rest where peace prevails.

We can take time in our day to visit the place of peace. We can clear a spot within our soul where love is the only thing welcome, for in the presence of love, the war comes to a halt. In the presence of love, conflicts fade in the distance. We can create an environment of love within us and outside us, and enjoy the temporary moments of peace that life guarantees to us. For even in turmoil there is precious peace for those who live by faith, trust, and love.

Lyndon B. Johnson said that peace is a journey of a thousand miles, and it must be taken one step at a time.

Thought of the Day

Even the insignificant sounds around us can be soothing and can restore peace for those who listen in silence.

When was the last time you took a bubble bath and listened to the crackling sounds of the bubbles? Remember how soothing and relaxing it made you feel? Remember the knots of emotions as they unwound with every crackle? Were you restored to your full emotional capacity by the experience?

Thoughts are like bubbles in the wind. We can have fun with them, knowing when to pop them and when to let them run their course. It's useless to hold on to them, for if we try to do that, they're already gone.

Listening without interpreting to the natural sounds of your environment is an effective way to restore the peace and tranquility of your soul. Try it today.

Thought of the Day

The mind is God's playground, and we can strive to keep it that way.

Some say the mind is the devil's playground, and the heart belongs to God. For a while, I embraced that thinking. It was the excuse I used when things went wrong; it was easy to blame the devil. I finally realized that if I lived according to that concept, I opened the door for the devil to feed my mind with his gifts of hate, jealousy, prejudice, and greed.

Since the mind is the point of entry before things get to the heart, it was impossible for me to receive the gifts of God when I believed my mind was the devil's playground. So that adage hasn't work for me, and today I'm going to change it.

I think it's important to operate from a position of strength not fear. I've positioned myself to receive love, peace, joy, and success. I will focus on making my mind God's playground.

WE ARE THE MOMENTS
WE ARE WAITING FOR

Thought of the Day

Everything that is present now is all we need for the perfect moment and perfect health.

Many times we think about things that aren't in our present moment. We try to solve problems that haven't manifested. Thinking of work while in bed doesn't make the bed more comfortable. It only confuses the mind and may even cause emotional discomfort. The better thing to do is to focus on your body as it adjusts to the comfort of the bed. Flex your toes, then your feet, then your knees, then your hips, then your shoulders. Dance, stretch, and breathe.

We can ensure that we are savoring the moments. We can breathe in consciously as we take in the moment. And as we stay focused on the present, we can experience the beauty of the moment.

Thought of the Day

Life comes only one moment at a time—not weeks, not days, just one moment. So use each moment wisely.

When our emotional troubles seem to come in bundles, we can step back in the moment and get a grip on ourselves. We can change that moment and avoid the slide into negativity. We can be thankful for the moments ahead and turn even the negatives into positives.

If we find ourselves constantly battling emotional turbulence, we might be letting our mind wander on negative things in our future. Zig Ziglar said that positive thinking allows us to do everything better than negative thinking.

Just for today, sit on the positive side of life. Welcome the wave of positive emotions as they wash up on your shores.

Thought of the Day

We are more than enough. Let's focus on those reassuring words.

We have come this far on our journey, walking through the storms of life that fed us fear one spoonful at a time. We've walked through the storms that told us we were inadequate and that we wouldn't make it. But look how far we've come. Now we can decide how far we want to go.

Now is the moment to change the false narratives and embrace the beauty of life in its abundance and entirety. Now is the moment to smell the roses and listen to the chirping birds. Now is the moment to witness the awakening of nature. Now is moment to reject anything that stands in the way of our breath of fresh air.

We can tell our fears that we are more than enough and that we're here to embrace the beauty of life.

Thought of the Day

Life is an experience of moments, so make each one special.

When we clear our mind of all thoughts, we achieve thoughtlessness. We experience life in the moment, and our emotions are restricted to the things of the moment. If we experience life in the now, we don't need to carry thoughts. Life is reduced to an experience of moments.

The important thing is our ability to cleanse ourselves from the turmoil of negative emotions. To get the most out of the moment, attend to your emotional needs. Spend time shedding negative emotions from within you.

Ultimate change begins with our perceptions. We tend to make decisions based on past experiences narrowed down to individuals in the form of stereotypes, and we create our own stereotypical experience in doing so. Then we miss the true essence of the individual in the present moment.

We can see each other today as though we were starved of yesterday. If we do, we will love with an authentic love without preconceived notions. We will love strangers as strangers without adding labels that cause us to choose between loving and not loving. When we do, we enhance each moment.

Thought of the Day

If we look closely, we can find happiness in the things around us. All we have to do is gravitate toward them.

When was the last time you stared in amazement at a beautiful morning sunshine and allowed it to soak into your soul? Did you feel the soft, radiant warmth of the morning rays? Did you notice the crystal rainbow of rays over the shades of your eyelids? Did you notice the chirping of the birds? When was the last time you danced to your favorite song all by yourself?

If we aren't in tune with life, there's a good chance we'll miss out on the happiness around us. We can take the time to dance by ourselves, sing out loud, smell the roses, bask in the morning sunlight, and listen to the chirping of a nightingale.

Thought of the Day

God doesn't promise us anything but death, but he gives us life as a gift.

Do you look forward to the day when you can walk into a store and say to a salesperson, "I've come for the big-screen television that God promised me?" Well, sorry to burst your bubble, but it's not going to happen. The only certain promise of God so far is death, until we find a way to live eternal.

In the meantime, God has given us the gift of life. The way we use this gift is up to each of us. Some embrace peace and harmony. Some are easily ticked off and quick with an angry word, and may even start a conflict.

Just for today choose peace over conflict.

Thought of the Day

We shouldn't let our yesterdays trap us in feelings of regret, because in our present joy, we have no recollection of yesterday. We've moved on, and so should others.

Should we spend precious moments thinking of people who've done us wrong? Should we secretly hope that their world will come crashing down? Unfortunately, in doing so, the only world we're destroying is our own. When we ignore the blessings of the present to try to gain revenge, all we succeed in doing is sabotaging our present joy. We become prisoners of the past that we so badly want to get over. Life moments are too short to be wasted.

Dr. Tony Evans said, "Don't let yesterday mess up today, which will ruin tomorrow." Just for today, stick with the joy that is presented to you, and enjoy it to the fullest.

Thought of the Day

A lazy mind may keep us stuck in the distant past, and we may miss the bus that carries our future.

We should say what we want to say and move on, for our thoughts can grow heavy and burdensome for those who waste time, and it takes energy to ponder against the waves of the past. Things come and go way too quickly to make sense of moments not understood, and they come around time and time again until we finally get it. The sooner we get it, the less likely we will need future lessons. Life can be a teacher for the unlearned, and the wise grasp wisdom from life.

We can make peace with our past so it won't be at war with our future.

WE ARE RENEWED
WITH EVERY BREATH

Thought of the Day

The cross position reveals the condition of our lives. Try it sometime. Spread your arms wide, hold your head upright, and breathe.

When we breathe deep enough and hold our breath long enough, we can correct a lot of things that aren't right with our being.

Life can be compared to a ship sailing on a breath of air. The smoother the breath, the smoother the ride. Each breath should cause smooth sailing.

Jeanette Leblanc says, "The audacity is in the living, not in the choosing. You are fearless enough to keep breathing in the face of loss and pain and humility and gratitude and gifts and brilliance and confusion. This is the amazing thing. Right or wrong can never be everything but small things in the face of your gigantic, intrepid spirit."

When life feels like you are caught up in storms, take a deep breath, hold it in, then release it slowly.

Thought of the Day

We can see the beauty of God's work all around us. But only when we close our eyes, shut our ears, and seal our lips, and breathe deeply can we embrace the presence of God within us and experience his magical works of healing.

In his book *Eight Shifts for Wellness*, Marc B. Levin writes, "You can use deep breathing to create an environment in your body favorable to healing."

When we hustle and bustle to the point where we never spend quiet moments acknowledging the presence of God within us, we increase our stress level and our risk of fatigue and illness.

If you feel sick or burned out, take twenty minutes or maybe a few hours to yourself for solitude. Make yourself comfortable, close your eyes, breathe deeply. Repeat the process as many times as necessary to restore your health. When you breathe deep enough and hold your breath long enough, you can correct a lot of things that are not right with your being.

Thought of the Day

Real peace can be experienced in a moment of silence when every barking emotion has receded into a position of submission to silence.

Real peace can be experienced when we clear the path for our breath to flow freely and uninterrupted.

Real peace can be experienced when we listen to the mass movement of air through our breathing.

When we focus on things that disturb our peace of mind, we are living in anticipation of our future. We can close our eyes with no thoughts and listen to the sound of our breathing, and in that way, we can erase all other thoughts and engage in real peace.

Thought of the Day

The God that brings us peaceful rest by night will never abandon us by day.

Who do you turn to when you awake on mornings? Who are you embracing to protect your newfound peace? Are you leaving your peace to embrace the medium that feeds your fears? Are you uncovering the dead fears of yesterday and bringing them alive each day?

When we find ourselves waking up with the fears of yesterday, we are trying to relive the past. It is best to clear our mind of yesterday's thoughts and to focus on the present moment.

Every day God gives us a chance to be renewed. What we do with that renewal is up to us? Do we love each other? Do we fall victims to the agendas of hate? Whether it's from the media or a person, every word comes into our path with the intent that we receive them. If our intent is love, anyone pushing hate will be exposed by the authenticity of our love. If the agenda is fear, anyone pushing fear will be exposed by the innocence of our love.

Just for today, we can promise ourselves that we won't be consumed by anything other than love.

6

COMMUNICATION IS
THE KEY TO SANITY

Thought of the Day

When we communicate with another, we can respond as though we are communicating to a best friend.

Be quick to pay a compliment, and make it the best one possible. Be quick also to apologize if a response comes across as insensitive. We shouldn't leave things up to the imagination of the receiver if we feel convicted in our heart or our soul of wrongdoing.

I got a shock when I commented on a friend's post on social media, not realizing that the post had come from him. As I evaluated my response, I felt it sounded insensitive, so I sent an apology to him. Fortunately, he didn't see my response as insensitive. He told me that his skin was not that thin. That incident made me realize that I should treat all my responses with that level of sensitivity.

When we feel convicted by our response to others, the best action we can take is to apologize and then move on.

Thought of the Day

A war in a heart serves no purpose other than to destroy the heart. A war in a mind serves no purpose other than to destroy the mind. A war in a soul serves no purpose other than to destroy the soul.

We should speak our truth and let it go. We should receive our truth and let it go. We can clarify our misunderstandings and let it go. Life is a collection of experiences too numerous to hold on to, for in holding on we bottle up our emotions. This obstructs the flow of beauty from the outside while destroying the beauty that's inside us.

According to Familydoctor.org, people who are emotionally healthy are in control of their thoughts, feelings, and behaviors. We can let go of negativity and usher peace into our world today.

Thought of the Day

Like them or not, opinions help us grow. But what good is an opinion if it's kept secret? An opinion expressed is better than an opinion suppressed.

Listen carefully to the response your opinions bring from others. Be willing to clarify what you meant by your opinions when asked to.

Seeking clarity before responding to a question can lead to understanding and great friendship. It can also lead to growth.

We all have views on many issues. When we lose patience with each other and block each other out, we no longer progress. We may not agree on everything, and that's okay, but dialogue is a good step toward progress and understanding. When we value our opinions to the point that we fail to listen to what others have to say, we are being selfish. It's best to listen with patience and show respect, even to those we disagree with.

Just for today, engage with someone with different views than you, and seek understanding with respect, patience, and love in your heart.

Thought of the Day

We can shape and change the world in whatever way we choose. The danger exists when we refuse to try.

As in a game of chess, we all try to make the world the place that will be the best for us. It's very likely that the changes we advocate are different from even those who are dear to us. Even as we play our opponents in this magnificent game of life, it's important that we respect each other.

Let civility, not anger, drive us to our cause. Understand the emotional stress that comes along with the fear of losing and the agony of defeat. Know that victory is not permanent and that how we treat each other in defeat determines how we are treated when we face our own defeat.

Play with passion. Laugh along the way. Make friends along the way. Grow along the way. And remember there is more growth in defeat than in winning. Nevertheless play to win, and don't forget to thank your opponents for a game well played, for even the game of life is temporary.

Be graceful to others, and that grace will return to you.

Thought of the Day

The perfect response is not necessarily the one that we agree with, but the one that opens a new way of thinking. Sometimes it's necessary to think long and hard before we give a response.

In a way, we're all Supreme Court justices. Some take their position more seriously than others. Some weigh the pros and cons. Some check for biases. Some flip the coin to see how it appears from the other side. Some let it come right out without a thought.

When we respond to others with the intent of hurting their feelings, we are hurting ourselves in the process. It puts us on guard as we await their response, putting us in a place of insecurity. Whatever response we offer, we can ensure that it reflects the brilliance in us, not the worst in us. But be sure to be at peace with both outcomes.

Thought of the Day

When we see each other today as though we were starved of yesterday, we love each other with a hunger filled with genuine love and without preconceived notions.

Change begins with our perceptions. We tend to make decisions based on past experiences, such as viewing individuals in the form of stereotypes. We create our own stereotype experience in doing so, while missing the true essence of the individual in the present moment. When we stereotype others based on unpleasant experiences, we hold ourselves prisoners to those experiences and become emotional hostages. We can pause, take a deep breath, and decide not to engage in our preconceived thoughts.

When we see the *more* that we are capable of and not the *less* in ourselves and in others, and when we see each other without preconceived notions, we love strangers as strangers without adding labels that allow us to make decisions about whether to love or not.

Just for today, destroy your preconceived notions and embrace love freely.

We can never win an argument by arguing to win, for the one who diffuses an argument is the ultimate winner and peacemaker.

Sometimes a conversation may quickly escalate into a confrontation. With the rise of social media, it's easy to find ourselves in conversations with strangers, discussing politics, race, religion, sexuality, and so on. It's important that we seek to understand others rather than to dictate to them. We can look for common ground where we can agree with each other and end the communication on peaceful terms. Some friendships can evolve with those with different viewpoints once we show mutual respect.

Remember that life is too short to be stuck in war. We can keep shifting our perspective until we arrive at our peace.

There are God-given opportunities in everyone you meet. Find them, nurture them, and if all else fails, be at peace and move on.

Thought of the Day

If we don't seek understanding, we may live in misunderstanding.

Many times things are not as they seem. Many times our understanding of something said is not what the speaker meant. The best way to communicate understanding is to ask questions. We can ask questions and present our understandings so that we obtain clarity.

Everyone who feeds our thoughts has an agenda, and the only way to receive a message accurately is to ask questions. Is it a message of love, or is it a message of fear? Is it a message that frees us, or is it a message that entraps us?

When we find ourselves frustrated in our communication with others, we should stop, take a minute, and ask questions. That way we seek clarity. Some may be annoyed with our asking, and some may thank us for seeking clarity.

Keep asking, for the truth shall set us free. When we seek, we find. We will never be everything to everyone, but to those who see our value, we're everything.

Thought of the Day

We shouldn't wait for God to ask us, "What have you done?"

We can be proactive. We can identify the afflictions of our souls. We can know the guilt that aches in our hearts. We can identify the conditions of our mind, body, and soul. Push your afflictions into the care of God. Ask him to take it away. Ask him to remove the indigestions of your soul.

If our communication intake was similar to our food intake, almost of us would be overweight. We simply don't know when we have taken in enough information. The unhealthier and the more addictive the information, the tastier it is. We gobble up gossip. We embrace slander. We eat hate like it's a dessert. And then somewhere in our waking moments, God reveals the indigestion of our soul and asks us, "What have you done?"

But it doesn't have to be that way. We know when we've done wrong. We know when guilt ruffles our peace. Why wait until God calls? Why not take it to him in prayer?

We can take a break and clean up our communication environment. We can focus on communication that is good for our spiritual growth, and when we do, we may enhance our peace.

Just for today, be honest with yourself. Be proactive. Say this prayer: "God, I've consumed too much, and I'm deeply conflicted. I need my peace back. Take away the pain of my emotions. Take away the pain of my heart. Take away the pain in my soul. Renew my spirit so I may go in peace and be of good service to you and to humankind."

Thought of the Day

We are victims of our own emotional state, and it is important not to get consumed by the emotional state of others.

Life is filled with drama. One look at the news, and it's easy to see the mess we humans can create in a twenty-four-hour day. When we interact with others, we are exposed to their own emotional state of being. It's okay to be compassionate, but in the process, we should remain objective.

We must ask ourselves what behavior may have led people to their present circumstances. Was it a healthy behavior? Are they victims of their own doing? Do they need one-time help, or do we need to make their circumstances ours?

Whatever decision we choose, it's important that we maintain our peace of mind in the process of helping and that we take an objective look at each situation. Sometimes it's important to be plain spoken and help a person own up to drama and not be victims of drama. Sometimes empathy is the only thing of value we can offer someone.

We also can examine ourselves. We can ask ourselves what actions we take that cause conflict. We can then focus on correcting those actions and seeking a way out.

Thought of the Day

Many try to claim God, and in their failure, they walk away disappointed, dejected, wounded, and depressed. Then, in humility, they understand that God can't be claimed. God can only be experienced. And he is always present.

Can we claim the oxygen in the air? Can we claim the oceans? Can we claim the land? Can we claim the birds in the skies? Then why would we think we can claim God? God has made himself readily available to all who wants to receive him.

Do you feel the presence of God in your life? How you choose to do so determines your experience.

Each breath should bring us closer to God's presence. We can be hungry for the presence of God. We can see God in everyone we meet and in everything seen and unseen. We can breathe in the presence of God with each breath.

Thought of the Day

We can make it our duty to be true to ourselves at all times because God already knows our lies.

Our way may not always be pleasing to others. Some may not like our way of thinking. We may not share the same political views or racial biases. We may not like each other's brand of Christianity. We may not share the same religious views. We may not back the same sports team. We may each lean on our own personal philosophy.

The truth of who we are may lead us to awkward beginnings. We can use our awkward beginnings to arrive at a common understanding where we can accept our differences and live in harmony. We can focus on what we like about each other and not on what sets us apart.

Everything about our faith is deeply personal, no matter how it may seem to those looking on from the outside. Faith is not permanent. It sometimes disappears. It sometimes leaves us lost, but it is our responsibility to find it.

We can spend time in the presence of the things that renew and strengthen our faith. When we restore our faith, we are also restoring our health. We become broken when our faith is diminished. We become whole when our faith is restored. We can attend to our spiritual needs. We can understand that faith gives us confidence to walk through the storms of life with our heads held high. We should spend time renewing our faith every day.

7

UNRESTRICTED LOVE
BREATHES FREEDOM

Thought of the Day

When we love without resistance, we can conquer fear and become experts at love.

We can blossom through the hard times and turn them into good times, one breath at a time. In life, we're either breathing in love or we're building walls of resistance. When we build walls of resistance, we restrict our breathing and put our health at risk.

Our breathing frees us while our resistance builds up stress and keeps us imprisoned in an uncomfortable state of mind. When we freely embrace love, we open up our access to God's presence.

We can spread our arms wide, lift our heads, and breathe deeply. We can feel the rush of love as it flows within us. Become an angel of love today.

Thought of the Day

We can't get to the sunset by avoiding the storm.

True love is being able to live patiently and to survive the things we don't love, while embracing and maximizing the experiences of living in harmony with the things we do love.

Anyone who's been fed the image that marriage is a prince riding off into the sunset with a beautiful princess should take a refresher course in marriage. The story ends when the horse gets tired or when it reaches its destination.

The point is that the person that we happily dated is not the only person riding on the back of the horse. Plodding along on the ride are the undisclosed, unresolved issues of the past. But those issues are not reasons to stop loving. They require the deeper aspects of love that take us through the storms of marriage: patience, compassion, forgiveness, and humility.

There will be many rides into the sunset if we do what it takes to ride through the storms.

Thought of the Day

Loving our neighbor is not restricted to the person living in the house on the other side of the fence.

It starts with the neighborhood of our thoughts, our joys, our hurts, and our pains. They all need our kindness and forgiveness.

It continues with our ability to interact with people who may incite hate, both intentionally and unintentionally. It is in our ability to convey love in our quest for understanding. It is in our ability to engage people in the most daring, complicated issues of the day without fear of persecution or restriction. Loving our neighbor is the most rewarding part of life. It holds the secret to our expression of freedom, and it starts with a simple hello and ends with a simple thank-you.

Let's love our neighbor today.

Thought of the Day

When we know who we are, we can reject the labels that others try to attach to us.

What if we walk into a store and see beautiful clothing, and just before we make our purchase, we looked at the labels? We start processing whether the brand is good or bad, quality or poverty. Regardless of how magnificent the product seems to be, we can't give it full recognition because of the labels and stereotypes we sometimes perceive.

Consider how beautifully a flock of birds flies together. Notice the aura in the sound they make. Are they male, or are they female? Are their sounds a warning, or are they rejoicing? We can do research and give some meaning to their sounds. We can associate their sounds with a past experience and put a label on it. But if we do, the aura that was once mysterious and enjoyed just for its sound takes on a whole new meaning. It may still bring joy to our hearts, but depending on the outcome of our studies, it may bring fear.

Life is a journey of movements. Labels may be necessary, but they shouldn't be many. The labels that matter is *alive* and *dead*. And at some point, they connect with each other and become useless.

A more appropriate label and the only one we will ever need is love. For love has no limits, no boundaries, no expectations, no regrets, and no end. The great I Am who sent us has given us an unlimited supply of love. We can use it in abundance. We can shatter the labels that hold our spirit in captivity. When we love without limits, our soul dives into the depths of the oceans of life, where it can't be entangled in the nets on the shore.

Just for today we can shake off labels, throw love at every moment that confronts us, and soar in our new freedom.

8

LOVE MAXIMIZES WHEN WE MAXIMIZE MOMENTS IN AWE

Thought of the Day

When we embrace moments in awe and don't flee from them as from a heated stove, we experience the wonders of life.

We can embrace the moments in our lives and express our gratitude with thankfulness and love. Be thankful to those whose dedication to their creative gifts has brought us the enjoyment we seek in life—the musicians, the actors, the producers, the chefs, the service providers. Some moments I lose myself in my favorite music. Some moments I sit around, enjoying my family.

We have been misled for so long and bombarded by fear for so long that we are afraid to savor the moments of life. We lose our awareness of the things around us, our environment, and our people.

We live in anticipation of the next experience that will confirm our fears. We give life to our fears while ignoring our experience of love.

When is the last time we stepped outside and expressed a sense of awe and gratitude for the things around us—for the morning air or the sight of someone new?

When we express love, and live in love, we enhance love. When we embrace fear, and live in fear, we magnify fear.

When we pray for love, we magnify love. When we pray about our fears, we magnify our fears. Pray love and thankfulness today, and experience the rush of life-changing love.

Thought of the Day

We can be thankful for every gift God has given us. Though it may not seem like a lot, it will multiply when we release it into the universe.

When our gift is in harmony with our kindness, it may change one person's life for the better. There is no greater power in this world than the power of human kindness. There is no greater destructive power in this world than the power of human unkindness.

Human kindness builds our heavenly experience, while human unkindness builds our hellish experience. We get to affect each person's existence through our actions. So choose wisely. The universe is watching. The universe is responding. You owe it to yourself to make this journey through life a good experience—not only for you, but also for others.

Thought of the Day

Love is of no use when it's deactivated. Let the light of the new day activate your love. Let your activated love be a light that shines love on others.

One of the things I love about life is receiving kindness from strangers. We were on a flight from Texas to California, and my wife was sick after a bout of food poisoning. She flew all the way with a plastic bag in her hand and took numerous trips to the restroom. The passenger on the aisle seat next to her reached out to us, offering ginger ale, extra napkins, and comforting words.

She was a shining light in our gloomy world. And this stranger dominated my prayers of thankfulness to God weeks after the event?

Her love was activated, and it reminded me of the essence of life. We possess a magic wand of love, and when we wave it at others, we make a difference in the world. We light up the world in dark places, starting with the simple things, like a smile, a hello, or holding the door for someone. We can do it. We can activate our love.

Thought of the Day

When we know what we're looking for, we know when we get it. The challenge is knowing how to nurture it.

Be mindful of those you love, and always seek to improve on love. Never take love for granted.

My name is Love, and my heart is bigger than any fear. My heart is bigger than any sorrow. My heart is bigger that any hurt. My heart is bigger than any pain. My heart is bigger than any act of unkindness. My heart is bigger than any hate. My heart is bigger than any injustice. My heart is bigger than any act of terror. My heart is bigger than any act of war. My heart is bigger than discrimination.

My name is Love. And God is the only source of love that I know. When others receive me, they should be receiving him. If they don't, I am not being authentic.

I know I'm not perfect, but I'm always in contact with the source of love. One day I will get it right. It's my hope for you and for me. My name is Love, and so is yours.

Thought of the Day

If God said, "I am," then his works say, "It is."

We all are the result of God's works in this temporary journey called life. Do we really get the choice to criticize the Maker's work as good or bad when we are just a minute, momentary part of the whole experience?

The only certain promise of God so far is death until we find a way to live eternally. In the meantime, God has given us the gift of life. The way we use this gift is up to each of us. Some people love peace and harmony, so they try to avoid war. They don't always succeed, but they try.

Some people are easily pissed off and are quick with an angry word. They could start a war in a minute. That's sometimes me, but not all the time.

The truth is like the song "Ebony and Ivory" by Paul McCartney and Stevie Wonder. There is good and bad in everyone, just like there is daylight and darkness in every day. We just have to find the balance.

Whatever way we choose to use the gift of life, we know the results of our thinking immediately, as they manifest themselves in our spirit through either joy or pain. We can choose joy in our day as much as possible.

Thought of the Day

In the wisdom of God, none of us is an expert, so we can understand his forgiveness, forgive ourselves, forgive others, and move on.

When God promised to give us an infinite amount of forgiveness, he probably did that because he knew the challenges we would face daily to get the condition of our heart, mind, body, and soul right so we could receive and distribute his love.

Every day we faced new challenges, and we share our opinions of what is right and what is wrong. Every day we put ourselves in positions to criticize the Creator's work, and then we pray that he makes changes.

What if we sought understanding without criticizing? What if we honored the gift of our existence and honored the existence of others? And what if we went about each moment with thankfulness for the things we understand and the things we don't understand?

What if, when we consider coming to our final bus stop on our journey, we know we will thank the driver and passengers we're leaving behind? Life would take on a whole different meaning.

Thought of the Day

A gift is not a gift unless it is given freely and lovingly. Until then it's just a burden that eats us up on the inside.

Give what God has given to you freely, and bless the world. The world needs your blessings. It is the only way to experience your importance and to make your mark in this handbook of the history of life. Give love, and love will set you free.

Love is the only food that feeds the heart, and it can be experienced only in giving of love. The more we give love, the more we receive love. As love flows from us, the fountain of life pours abundant love into us.

Eckhart Tolle said that whatever you think the world is withholding from you, you are withholding from the world.

Give some love today.

Thought of the Day

Failure to act is the basis of many of life's regrets.

In a way, we're all on the stairway to a heavenly existence, and from time to time, life tugs at our heartstrings, encouraging us to lend a hand to someone who needs it. We know it when we experience it. When we do, we shouldn't hesitate to act. Failure to act is the basis of life's regrets. Regret is a miserable place to exist. It eats at the fabric of the soul while spinning our lives into turmoil and guilt.

Imagine what life will be like when we look after the needs of our neighbors during their trying times. We will prevent many of tragedies.

When we become the light in someone's darkness, we brighten our world.

9

SMILES PAINT THE WORLD HAPPY

Thought of the Day

Your smile is like a painter's brush that enhances the painting with every stroke. With it you can change your world one person at a time.

Can you remember the last time you smiled at a stranger for no reason other than being happy you were both on this journey through life? Did you thank God for that person's presence?

A smile opens the windows to a soul, and it welcomes love from a distance. A smile sets the tone for the day ahead. It's the perfect investment in an exceptional day.

Take time to smile today and experience the magnitude of love that will circulate and gravitate toward your present moments.

Thought of the Day

If we treat everyone we meet as though we've seen a superstar, we will be star struck and smiling.

From time to time while shopping, I look at fellow shoppers with looks of excitement, the kind of look I'd give someone when I recognize that he or she is a superstar. Many times the shoppers' faces light up, and they return a smile. Of course, there are others who just ignore me. Those who smile make the whole experience worth it. Their smiles stay with me throughout my day. Their smiles keep me smiling.

Just for today, we can see the people that we meet as superstars, treat them that way, and feel the difference it brings to our lives.

Thought of the Day

Our lives are the greatest toys we'll ever have, and they are always changing.

The one common factor that makes life work is our breathing, so we should make each breath an enjoyable experience. During stressful moments, it is easy to forget to breathe. It's easy to get consumed by stress. In the process our chest constricts, and we feel discomfort. But we shouldn't have to live with the discomfort. We can turn our focus back to our breathing. We can clear our mind of thoughts and focus on regulating our breath. We can step back and smile at ourselves.

The things in life we have no control over can be taken with a smile, and the things in life we have control over can be given with a smile. In this circle of life, we are only as strong as our weakest link.

Just for today, reach out and strengthen someone.

Thought of the Day

When we grow our purpose with utmost love and compassion, we may raise up a generation with love and compassion. Remember that every person matters, and those closest to us mean everything.

If I haven't say in my silent moments, "Jesus, I love you," I haven't expressed gratitude to the source of my love. If I haven't smiled in silence for the love I feel for my wife, I probably haven't loved enough. If I don't smile in silence for the love and life of my children, I'm probably taking their existence for granted. If I don't smile in silence over a friend, I'm probably undeserving of friendship.

Purpose recognizes all things, and there is purpose in all things. As we grow in our purpose, we expand the horizons of healing in the world. We become the healers of broken things.

When we lead with purpose, we grow our generation with purpose. If we lead with recklessness, all we succeed in doing is grooming a reckless generation.

When we speak words of love, love returns to our generation and us in more ways than we can imagine.

Today I honor loving fathers and wives and friends, and I honor God in the process.

We are not the message. We are the messengers.

So many times, we find ourselves packaging the message. We house it in mansions. We decorate it in songs. We secure it in fancy cars and clothing. We embody it in holiness, and we become the message, not the messenger. We then treat the message like it is the messenger.

We distort love and repackage it to mean what we want it to mean. We show love to some and not to others. We package love in different skin types, sexual preferences, or religions. We become experts at repackaging the message, and then we sell it to others at an enormous price: the price of their soul.

There will be a time when the message confronts us and puts us in our rightful place. It reminds us that the message is love, and it is better and sincerer in its natural environment.

Go out and spread love into the world today. Send a smile to someone. Brighten someone's day. Be the difference. Reflect authentic love. Be the messenger, and let love be the message.

10

EXPERIENCE AN EMOTIONAL MAKEOVER

Thought of the Day

The greatest gift we can give ourselves is an emotional makeover, and the only requirement is our attentiveness and action.

If God is the source of our love, why are we withholding it from ourselves? Are we living in the full potential of our love? Are we happy? Are we feeling the bliss of love? Many of us depend on others to fulfill our need for love. We are disappointed when things don't work out the way we want them to. We blame others for shortcomings. We make demands on them.

Sure, people mess up at times, but the real test of love is the love we give ourselves. Our soul has a hunger for love just like our hunger for food, drinks, and oxygen. Our lack of love sometimes shows up as emotional pain and a loss of blissfulness.

When we start loving ourselves, we notice radiance returning to our lives, and it permeates into the lives of our spouses, children, and pets.

So how do we love ourselves? We start by staying emotionally connected to God. We develop workout routines. We do stretches, breathe deeply, and speak only positive words over our lives. Then we can love others.

Just for today, we can choose to unleash the source of God's love in our lives.

Thought of the Day

It is okay to experience emotional pain, but it isn't okay to leave it unattended.

As long as we experience life, we will experience emotional turbulence brought on by our personal challenges and the challenges facing our world, such as our finances and acts of terrorism. We may not be able to change the outcome of these challenges, but we can use the time to attend to our responses to them.

If we feel sad, we can love on ourselves. If we feel angry, we can embrace humility. We can forgive ourselves then accept ourselves. Much anger is born out of rejection. If we feel defeated, we can pump ourselves up for one more shot at victory. Heroism is born out of snatching victory from the jaws of defeat.

Feeling helpless? Call on the name of Jesus. Allow him to be the comforter of your soul.

Our security comes when we renew our hearts daily in the presence of God.

If you felt secure yesterday, will you receive an automatic certificate of renewal today? No. Feeling secure is a process of renewal. It requires temporarily removing ourselves from material things and standing empty of thoughts, of wants, and of needs in the presence of God. This is a heart-felt connection that allows a cleansing process. It is a fresh start. It gives us the ability to see with new eyes. It gives us the opportunity to love ourselves so we can love others. We can spend quiet times renewing our minds, bodies, and souls.

Thought of the Day

Thankfulness is the one prayer that God answers instantaneously.

The most important prayer we'll ever pray is "Thank you, God." I believe there are healing powers in prayers of thankfulness. They require trust in God, knowing that his will is done. We can trust that whatever the outcome in life, God is looking out for us.

When we pray, "Thank you," we reinforce a feeling of gratitude throughout our body. Every part of our being embraces the message, and we experience a feeling of transformation from negativity to positivity.

I've prayed for many things in my life. I've prayed to be rich. I've prayed for a house and a car. I've even prayed to win the lottery. Sometimes God takes quite a while to answer my prayers, and it baffles me. I think that if I were God, all it takes is for me to wave the magic wand and all prayers will be answered. Then it dawns on me that an all-powerful and all-knowing God knows my needs, and therefore there is no need to ask.

So I pray for thankfulness, and with each prayer I experience a lift in my heart and the joy of gratitude. With each prayer of thankfulness, God brings the light of his love to my heart, and the darkness disappears. Thankfulness is the only prayer I've gotten an immediate response to.

Just for today, we can repeat a prayer of thankfulness throughout our busy moments.

Thought of the Day

Life can be a delicacy when we put its ingredients to good use.

Life by itself is as meaningless as an apple sitting on a counter, surrounded by the ingredients for an apple pie, but rotting away. The delicacy comes together when we stir up all the ingredients, intermingling them with each other to create an irresistible pie.

The ingredients for an apple pie don't change, and the success of the pie depends on the amount of the ingredients used. Each ingredient must be used in its rightful quantity.

So, what ingredients are we going to use in our apple pie today? Is it family? Is it friendship? Is it dialogue? Is it music? Is it the breath of life? Is it relaxation? Is it faith? Is it peace? Is it in harmony, with all the above engaging in a deeper experience? Whatever ingredients we choose, we can add a good dose of love in the mix and remember to share a slice.

We are the final product of the ingredients we feed into our lives over time. If we don't add an ingredient, it will be missing in the final product.

The new day gives us a chance to master the recipe of our lives, so we can share a great life experience with others. We can ensure that the pie puts a smile on the face of those who receive it.

11

UNITY IS STRENGTH

Thought of the Day

God is love, and love can be attained only in unity and harmony with the diverse many.

A lake always seems unified until the ripples of a pebble send its parts fleeing, but it always comes back to a place of calm. We humans tend to flee each other with acts of violence. We assume that acts of violence are clear indications that we can't live with each other.

But do you know that the pebble that destroys the peace of the lake ends up at the bottom of the lake, where it too finds peace? Do you know that its act didn't keep the lake in permanent disorder? Have you witnessed an ant trail terrorized by the hand of a human? The ants reform their trail in unity.

Life is challenging, and it works best when our unity is not broken by fear but mended by love. Let us keep the trail of love in unity with each other.

Thought of the Day

Without justice, there is no love. But what is justice without love?

A potential friend may appear to be an enemy if we receive that person as an enemy. Be slow to anger, and look for love in every situation. This is the common ground we all long for even as we seek justice. But what is justice without love?

What if there were really a handbook of life, and those who died got to write in the book a recollection of how they got to the place of death? What if it was the only book God read? What would the truth reveal? Would it reveal a violent death? Would it reveal a sacrificial death? Would it reveal a death caused by an inhumane act of another?

What if through our daily prayers and gratitude we are writing in the handbook of life? Would God be reading stories of our hatred for one another? Would he read of our greed? Would he read of the good someone poured into our lives or the good we poured into someone's life? Could it be that love for one another makes the best stories for a loving God?

Thought of the Day

Belief is the most powerful gift we can give ourselves.

It can be an honor to believe in love and to tell those who are struggling with love that we believe in them rather than kicking them to the curb.

It can be an honor to tell people that though we've never seen them, we believe in their inner beauty. It can be an honor to tell people that though we've never heard them speak, we believe in their ability to achieve greatness. It can be an honor to tell people that though we've never sat in their concert, we believe in their magnificence. It can be an honor to tell people that though we've never seen God, we believe in every word of his utterance. But if we believe we should act in our true understanding of what his words mean to us, those words may not mean the same to others.

We can be tolerant in our pursuit of life and adhere to our high standards and those of others.

Thought of the Day

Now that we know we're all human, let us love each other.

Let us welcome each other. Let us celebrate our differences. Let us lift each other up. Let us learn from each other. Let us honor the work of our Father in each other and know that he did a good thing, even if his work is too complicated for us to comprehend. Let us know that his intent is love, and it is the one gift we all possess.

Be sure that the things you're giving are adding beauty to the world and not taking it away. Let us focus on the positives and not the negatives. Let us stand in each other's corner and work in harmony with each other, weathering the storms of life. If we do, we may succeed in making the world a better place.

Thought of the Day

Life is a balancing act between good and bad.

We can be too good and too bad, just like a night-and-day experience. We're all going around in the circle of life.

We have our religion, and we know what it says to do and not do. But when it's crunch time, true religion is the sum of a person's morals. Each person's morals are different from the other person's morals, and moral values change as we learn.

The challenge we face is how to make life work for the good and the bad in each of us while creating harmony for all. The answer? One person at a time solves one problem at a time.

Thought of the Day

We have the gift of the Holy Spirit, which begs a question: "What will God do in our current situation?" He guides us to act appropriately. He brings joy to our heart when our actions bring joy to another person's heart. And he just as easily convicts us when our actions are contrary to the spirit of love.

I once met a homeless couple at a laundromat as they came in to do their laundry. They sat in the area where I normally dry my clothes. I thought about using a different area to dry my clothes, but then I asked myself, *What would Jesus do in this situation?*

I did what I normally do. I walked into the area they were sitting in with my clothes to dry. We got into the most amazing conversation I have ever had. Race didn't matter in our conversation. Immigration status didn't matter. Religious status didn't matter. They knew me based on my actions. I encouraged them and rejoiced with them. At the end of the encounter, I blessed them financially.

I've never felt so good having interaction with people who were just living their lives and knowing that they were down but not out.

Thought of the Day

The most important stop in life is the one we fear the most.

We can pour love onto a situation where hate exists. I once had an experience in which the person sitting in the most visible area of my place of worship was in a wheelchair. He didn't smile, and he looked uncomfortable. He didn't look in my direction when I passed his way, so I assumed he wanted to be left alone.

In my mind, the spot he occupied became the left-alone spot. It was the most uncomfortable spot for me.

Then God spoke to my heart about the role I was playing in creating this uncomfortable spot in his place of worship. So, that Sunday, I walked straight to the spot where he was strapped in his wheelchair and introduced myself. I told him how special he was to me. He shook my hand firmly, and then we shared a hug.

That moment transformed the most uncomfortable spot in the room to the most loving spot in the room. He no longer sat in church as a victim of a tragedy. He was the most important spot, and everyone gravitated to his spot, including me. He now sits proudly in his wheelchair, looking forward to worship with a smile on his face.

I learned a very important lesson that day. Before I contribute to my hatred, however small or big it is, I can throw love on it. Love always win.

Thought of the Day

There is Jesus in everyone we meet.

Before we criticize or judge someone, we need to find the Jesus in that person and thank God for giving us the opportunity to meet him in his different forms.

Yes, Jesus is in the broken. He was broken, and the very humanity he came to save rejected him in his brokenness. Today the brokenness of Jesus shows up in all different forms of life. Though we may not condone someone's lifestyle or behavior, we don't have the right to criticize or judge him or her.

Sometimes we act as though God is sitting in a wheelchair, watching the world self-destruct. The opposite is true: we're the ones sitting in wheelchair mode, watching the world self-destruct. Humankind has solved the greatest problems in life, but some problems go on for economic reasons, even when it costs lives. Can we name a few? Wars, abortion, poverty, greed?

We can accomplish great things when we recognize the good in humanity and reach out to others even when all we see is the bad. This will allow us to reach common ground to solve some historic problems.

Thought of the Day

Whatever dominates our hearts will dominate our heaven or our hell.

There are consequences for every word uttered, kind or unkind. There are consequences for every deed done, good or bad. Victory today doesn't guarantee victory tomorrow. Failure today doesn't guarantee failure tomorrow. But love guarantees love—love of self and love of neighbors. Who deserves love? Everyone.

We all came from God's creation. We don't get to choose who deserves love, though we may try. We may even convince ourselves that we're doing the right thing by holding back our love from others. After all, holding back love hurts us in a pleasant way. Revenge feels good, but just for a little while. Unfortunately, the cycle of revenge goes on for many generations to come. Just look at the wars in the world; some of the wars that were fought in biblical times are still boiling hot.

Haven't we learned? Is history not proof enough that whatever we're doing is not working?

Only love can free us from this madness, and it starts within the heart of each of us.

Thought of the Day

The greatest expression of love comes through our compassion for others.

We can feel the presence of God through our compassion. Jesus said when two or more are gathered in his name, he is present. Compassion is not a singular experience. Jesus will always be present in our moments of compassion. Why? Because compassion is our greatest expression of love, and Jesus is love.

Every day brings new opportunities for us to connect with each other in a deep, meaningful way, and we can experience the magnitude of our connection when we bring our compassion to the forefront. Don't miss an opportunity to show or receive compassion.

Compassion heals the heart of all wounds. We need to be sure we are living in the spirit of compassion toward others.

12

COMMITMENT IS
THE KEY TO LOVE

Thought of the Day

Ask not what God can do for us, but what we can do for others.

Our perception is that God is here to serve us as opposed to us being here to serve each other. We pray for the things we want from God, and we thank him for the things that are going well in our lives. We get impatient with him when things are going slow, and we get angry with him when things are going wrong.

Meanwhile, God is probably looking at us like a parent looks at a child, smiling when we start our first crawl, applauding when we take our first step, and rejoicing when we become adults and fend for ourselves while looking out for others.

Thought of the Day

Focus on what you can do for others, not on what others can do for you.

It's easy to be held prisoner to self-pity and feelings of not belonging, but it's freeing to focus on how we can contribute without focusing on belonging.

When we focus on contributing in whatever situation we find ourselves, we overcome the pressure of feeling a need to belong or be accepted. By contributing, we make a difference in the lives of others, and we experience the rewards of our input. Our contributions elevate us from a position of dependence to one of empowerment. They shift us from a position of feeling frustrated about the things we want to experience but aren't experiencing to a position of joy for the things we are bringing into other people's lives.

Just for today, let's focus on what we can do for others, not what others can do for us.

No one heals a wound by hammering a nail through it, and no one heals a relationship by hammering an argument into it.

Relationships may go through seasons of highs and lows, but commitment isn't seasonal. Commitment is staying together through the good and the bad and having the patience and tolerance to see it through to the other side of the rainbow.

Two people can survive a marriage if one person is wounded emotionally to the point that he or she is angry, if the other person is grounded emotionally so that he or she can listen beyond the emotions of anger and find peaceful solutions. Someone must be the one to apply a Band-Aid over the wound.

Two people cannot survive a relationship if both are angry. It will lead only to arguments and eventually defeat.

Someone should assume the role of peacemaker. This means remaining focused and patient. It doesn't mean allowing a partner to be disrespectful. We can tell people they're being disrespectful without being angry, and we don't have to reward disrespect, but we can strive for peace and harmony.

Thought of the Day

We can make people happy only by giving them what they want and not what we think they need. But we can only give them what they want if we can fulfill their wants.

Sounds weird, but let me explain. I went to the supermarket with my nine-year-old daughter. A man approached me and asked for ten dollars. He said he was hungry and needed the money to buy something from a restaurant next door. I didn't have change, so I asked if he would wait for me to get change from a cashier. Then a thought hit me: *If he's hungry, why don't I just buy something healthy at the supermarket?* I asked him, "How about some grapes?"

He looked at me puzzled. "I don't want grapes. I told you what I want."

I said, "Beggars can't be choosers," and offered to buy him any meal in the supermarket.

He replied, "Never mind. Keep your money."

As I shopped for my items, I asked my daughter if I had done the right thing in offering him food rather than money. She said I should have given him the ten dollars.

"But what if he wasn't hungry and was going to buy drugs?" I asked.

"You should have given him the money."

As we were leaving the supermarket, lo and behold, the man was waiting outside. Someone had just given him a couple of dollars, and then I handed him my ten. He smiled, apologized, and promised to put it to good use. Then he disappeared.

Today the thought became a little clearer for me as I wondered if my daughter was right. She didn't use all the analyzing I used; she just made her decision on impulse. And she was probably right. I didn't make him happy until I gave him what he wanted.

Thought of the Day

Be patient with the dark areas of life, for these too will see the light of day.

We can't love the dark the same way we love the light, for if we did, we may stumble and fall. Loving the dark entails patience, steps and missteps, stumbles, and sometimes falls. But darkness is temporary, even when it's necessary. When we face the darkness, it's best to slow down and move carefully through life as we ask God for guidance.

In our darkest moments, we experience the quickest growth, but it entails having the patience and persistence to understand and overcome the lessons of the dark.

We can commit to learn from the dark areas of our lives and be vigilant to embrace the first ray of hope.

Thought of the Day

Some things that challenge us in life only make us stronger when we refuse to accept defeat.

I play a game daily. I enjoy it, but that's not my motivation for playing. The real motivation is that I'm up against a player that beats me most of the time. I play this person over and over, and I see improvements on my end. I don't have a good win-loss ratio, but I'm improving. I'm grateful this player is patient with me and continues to play with me even when I lose badly. I try to be just as patient with those I beat.

When we face challenges, we may experience defeat, but as long as we don't walk away defeated, there's a chance we may overcome—or at least come out of it stronger and more experienced.

Thought of the Day

Our perceptions become our reality only when we don't seek clarity.

When we seek clarity, the answers may be revealed to us, but if not, at least we can say we tried.

So many times someone says something that offends us, and instead of asking for an explanation of their words, we walk away dejected. What if we misinterpreted what was said? By walking away, we deny ourselves the opportunity to bring clarity to the situation. We then form our own opinion of the person who offended us, and we make the problem bigger than it needs to be.

The easier thing to do is to ask for an explanation of what was said. Clarifying can turn a potential enemy into a lifelong friend.

Just for today, ask for an explanation of offensive words, and let it be an opportunity to strengthen your relationships rather than tear them apart.

Thought of the Day

The secret to a happy marriage is to learn to live with the side that isn't happy and not let it get in the way of your happiness.

Many people go into marriage with the Snow White concept of being swept away by the prince or princess and riding off in the sunset. They soon find out that even a horse has to stop for gas. Even a horse has to relieve itself. (There is nothing more disgusting than horse gas. Well, maybe a skunk, but no one rides a skunk. Horseback riding is fun, if we can handle the gas.)

I have my bad ways, and I enjoy them. I've learned to let my partner have her bad ways too. I just do damage control, cleaning up the mess as we go.

I read once that President Abraham Lincoln had a very bad temper. So before he sent out a telegram, his wife read it—and sometimes discard it without him knowing. It must have prevented a lot of wars.

Newlyweds, remember that the secret to a happy marriage is to discover your partner's bad side and learn to live with it. But, most of all, marriage is a lifetime commitment, not a sprint to the next block.

Thought of the Day

Marriage is based on commitment more than on love, but love is the fruit of a committed marriage.

Through the years, I've seen love come and go. I've treasured every moment of love, but what matters most to me is my commitment to my marriage. That commitment creates an environment for love to flourish and grow.

I've seen couples who love each other fall apart because they failed to commit to each other in areas such as love, money, and family. The failure to commit led to distrust and a lack of respect for each other. This ultimately led to the destruction of their marriage.

Commitment is the foundation of a good marriage. It's a challenge, but it's the essence of building good individual character, which can lead to a successful relationship.

Just for today, let's work on our commitment in relationship.

13

OBSTACLES ARE CATALYSTS FOR SUCCESS

If there were no obstacles in this game of life, no one would play.

When we welcome obstacles and then rise above them, there is nothing more fulfilling. Each obstacle we overcome pushes us to a new level of growth. Each obstacle that we fail to overcome stifles our growth. Either way, this game of life is a beautiful challenge.

Some days we win, and some days we lose. But what good is it to compete against an opponent that doesn't play at our skills level, thereby not challenge our ability to grow?

How do we meet the challenges of a great opponent? Do we run and hide? Or do we cry like a child? Do we surrender without a fight? Or do we give it all we've got until the very end?

Are we living with the confidence that God is always by our side? Do we feel better knowing that the opponent we're up against is powerless in the presence of the God we serve? Who is your opponent? Is it depression or grief? Is it sadness? Or is it fear? Is it regrets? Or is it missed opportunities? Is it anger? Or is it sorrow? Is it self-doubt? Or is it mental fatigue?

Just for today, promise yourself that you are up for the challenges of life, and bring on your A game.

Thought of the Day

Greatness travels difficult paths and endures difficult tests.

Years ago, in the early days of Elvis Presley's career, a music producer advised him to stick to truck driving. What if Elvis had taken his advice? What if he had given up on his dream?

Instead he got better and more creative with his music. He took chances that no one was taking at the time. He studied the art of rhythm and blues and understood the passion that made it great. And he became great.

Sometimes a dream killer is all you need to fuel your quest for greatness. When people say you can't, let it be your motivation to say, "I can."

Thought of the Day

On every step of this life's journey, we are children and we are parents. The child learns, and the parent teaches.

We can perform our duties diligently so that when we are in our twilight years, we can reflect on the fond memories of helping others reach their full potential and be forever thankful to those who helped us reach our full potential.

Be a parent today, but at the same time, explore your talents with the eager eyes of a child guided by the works of others who have gotten to where you want to go.

We are ready. The only time left is now. We've come too far to turn back now. We can become everything we were meant to be and fulfill our promises to God and self.

Thought of the Day

We can reinvent ourselves today if we don't like the rewards of yesterday.

Everyday life gives us the opportunity to revisit the day before and either embrace our path or make amendments or adjustments. We can view these changes when we know with clarity what we would like our future to look like. We are like architects designing our future. With God as our foundation, we can go forth and build the designs we foresee.

We may make mistakes along the way, but we can rise above mistakes and focus on our goal. We can view mistakes as a way to reinvent ourselves and persevere on the path that leads to and fulfills our vision of our future.

Thought of the Day

Sometimes God blocks our small doors so bigger doors can be opened.

Sometimes we spend our lives banging on the same door and getting the same results as we wait for change to come. Then, all of a sudden, we are removed from the situation, such as through a job loss. It may seem like a sink-or-swim moment, but the goal is to move us along to achieve greater things.

When small doors are blocked, instead of sulking, rejoice in anticipation of the big doors that are about to open. Know that God always has your back.

Thought of the Day

Every hurdle we experience has been experienced by someone prior to us and, in some cases, turned into an opportunity. All we need to do is research the hurdle and turn it into our own opportunity.

When we face hurdles, many of us gravitate toward fear. In fear mode, we close up and do everything we can to shelter ourselves from the hurdles. We avoid them instead of facing them head on and solving them the best way we can. Though hurdles may be obstacles, they provide us the opportunity to grow and overcome adversity. To overcome, we need to dig deep within ourselves and come up with the best possible solutions to move past the hurdle and turn it into an opportunity for great things.

Be mindful of fear, and replace it with positive thoughts that empower you to conquer your fears. When we do that, we are on the path to turning our hurdles into opportunities for success.

Thought of the Day

A wise person may see a problem and turn it into an opportunity. A selfish person may deny others an opportunity. A foolish person may see an opportunity and turn it into a problem.

Before we complain, we should look closer and be observant. Life's greatest opportunities sometimes show up as life's greatest problems.

Life is like a game that we may not always win, but we can learn from our opponents. Take the time to understand someone today. Ask a question that seeks understanding rather than giving an answer that reflects defeat.

To achieve anything great in life, our will to succeed must be greater than the hindrance of defeat. Every hindrance creates an opportunity for us to strengthen our will.

Thought of the Day

The two most important things we achieve in life are our goals and our distractions.

It's important to know what is a goal and what a distraction is at any given moment and treat it that way. Goals take us to higher levels of life, whereas distractions take us back to a lower level or leave us stagnant.

Make a list of your goals and your distractions, and monitor the time you give to each. Prioritize your time toward your goals, not your distractions, and you will be back on track to achieving success.

Life's journey is like a plane ride. If we don't know where we're going, we don't know where we'll arrive. Plan your journey carefully and be focused. Find a good copilot and a mechanic to make it work. Then put all your faith and trust in God to make it a reality.

Thought of the Day

Success has only one winner. It's either us or our distractions, and we get to choose.

Distractions are the only challenges we face in achieving success, and there are too many to mention. But we can overcome them if we remain focused. The question becomes "Are we up to the challenge?"

Success is a game of mental focus and toughness, and it comes with lots of practice.

The prize always seems to be shifting, but we can maintain our focus. We can recognize the things that are not of the prize and give them the least priority. We can prioritize the things that keep us on the path to achieving success.

The game of life has many opponents that act as distractions. In the Garden of Eden, the opponent was a serpent. In today's world, distractions are not as obvious as a talking serpent, but they are still obvious—dwindling finances, health issues, a rise in cost of living, computer games, social media. The challenge for us is how to avoid biting into our distractions and to stay the course that leads us to success.

Thought of the Day

Our greatest opportunities arise from our greatest adversities.

We've all experienced terrible things, but how many of us, if given a magic wand, would use it to erase the bitter past? I wouldn't. I believe my past has groomed me to be who I am today. I am happy with how I turned out. And I can use the terrible moments of my past as teachable moments to tell my story and help others along the way.

Booker T. Washington said that success is to be measured not so much by the position that one has reached in life as by the obstacles he has overcome. What are the obstacles standing in the way of your success? Are they slowing you down, or are they fueling your will to succeed? Each obstacle you face is an opportunity for growth. You can embrace it and grow gracefully and confidently.

The fire sent to consume us can be the fuel we use to propel ourselves to our next level of success.

When we face difficulties, we can remain calm and hold on to our faith, trusting that God has our best interest in mind and rejoicing in our commitment to see things through. If we find the patience to flourish through the droughts, we may reap the benefits when the rain falls.

Not knowing the outcome is not an excuse for not pursuing our dreams. God designed it so we may know that we reap the rewards of what we sow. We can do the work and follow our dreams, however simple they may seem to us, and let God provide the way.

Thought of the Day

Our testimony can free us from our past, and it can rescue those who are trapped in their present.

Sometimes our bad experiences hold more value than our good experiences. Our past is a treasure house of valuable memories—the good and the bad. We can tell our story the way we experienced it. It can be our pathway to freedom and great wealth.

We sometimes let our bad experiences hold us prisoner to the past. There isn't a thing in my past that I would go back and change, because it is the foundation of who I've become and who I strive to be.

The challenge we face is how to give life to the past so we can set it free. The best way to release the past is to tell our stories, to tell our testimonies to the right audience, though not everyone will connect to them.

When we tell our testimonies, we set our past free. And it may free others who are trapped in their present.

Thought of the Day

Those who challenge others' way of thinking open the way for growth of others and themselves.

It can be a good thing when our friends challenge us. It can be their way of showing that they care. We can welcome the challenge of a spouse for the same reason. We can avoid taking things personally. Though this may be difficult, holding a grudge because someone challenged us or treated us badly is more damaging to us than letting it go.

It takes a lot of energy to store ill feelings within us. It is freeing to let them go and move on, and that doesn't mean we're accepting the actions of others. It just means we won't internalize our emotions to the point that it affects us negatively.

Just for today, promise yourself to let go of all grudges and free your mind of negativity.

14

RISK IS THE ONLY RECIPE FOR SUCCESS

Thought of the Day

Those who live on the shores may not be the best ones to criticize those who live in the oceans.

Life's journey is like a swim in the ocean. It entails learning, enjoying, and mastering, and there are always risks. But risks weren't made to keep us from taking chances.

Risk is the essence of achieving greatness. It separates the sheep from the lambs. It gives us the option to live on the shore, but it doesn't give us the right to criticize those who head to the ocean. We can survey the oceans we've crossed before we survey the ocean others are crossing. The lessons we learn from our own ocean crossings can be valuable to those starting their journeys across the shores and into the ocean.

Thought of the Day

He who is not afraid to lose his way will always find his way.

If we've never been lost, we don't know what it's like to be found. Life is forever leading us to new paths. It's the way we grow. We tend to ignore the nudging of life. We tend to resist change. We embrace the things we're familiar with.

If we explore the new opportunities life presents to us, that ignites the growth process. We can make the decision to pursue growth or to change its course if we don't like where it's leading us. Our passion lets us know if the path we're following should be pursued or discarded.

If we followed our dreams and they amount to nothing, at least we dreamed.

Just for today, take a chance on a new path, and then make a decision on how far you're willing to grow.

Thought of the Day

Sometimes the only chance we'll have in life is the chance we take.

There's a thin line between success and failure. Success is all about risk taking. Risk doesn't guarantee success, but without risk, we will not achieve our goals.

Failure is not permanent, but many times it's part of the learning process. Think about it this way: An infant attempts its first step but fails. That doesn't stop the infant from attempting its second walk. Here's the trick though: There is a parent cheering the infant along. There is a parent rejoicing with the infant every step of the way. Then there is a community celebrating that infant's triumph. The questions then are, when did we stop taking chances? Who told us it is useless to try? When did we give up on our dreams? What will it take for us to get back on track fearlessly?

Who do we have in our circle? Are they encouraging us, or are they helping us kill our dreams? We can build the right team to cheer us on in our race. Today is the only day we may have to run our race.

Make ready, get set, and go. The race has begun. We've left the block. We're no longer stuck at the starting line; our only goal is to finish the race. Time is important. We can push to finish in record time and enjoy the fruits of our victory.

Thought of the Day

Only those who failed fail.

Are we challenging ourselves, or are we crippled by a fear of failure? Is fear eating away at our core as we stand at the sidelines, watching life go by while we hold our golden ticket safely tucked away? If our gifts never find an outlet, the only thing we may achieve is failure.

So what's brewing inside you? Can you find ways to express it? Can you find ways to expose it little by little and experience the excitement as it grows?

The first time I stepped out on stage as a stand-up comedian, the words I uttered didn't get further than the front row. I could see the annoyed people in the back frantically waving their hands in frustration.

I didn't want to be there. If I'd had my way, I would have never allowed myself to be talked into going on stage. I would have sat comfortably in my group as a writer, not a performer. I was frustrated by our group policy that said that if you wrote it, you had to perform it.

I remember the first time the audience laughed at one of my jokes. It was during my sixth outing. The laughter threw me off, and I forgot the rest of my lines. I silently cursed God that I'd made a complete fool of myself.

Luckily, I kept my lines in my back pocket. I flicked out my paper, glimpsed at the lines I forgot, and blurted out the ending. Then I got a standing ovation.

Later I toured with a group to Aruba and performed in an international theater festival. I had two lines in the play, but one of the actors forgot his line and caused us to skip a scene with one of my lines. My scene was a bar scene, and I accidentally sat with my back to the audience. The judges liked the idea and pointed it out in their review of our performance. They said it looked authentic. In my mind I was failing, but because I persisted, I didn't fail. It's only when we fail to persist that we fail.

Face your fears of failure. Align with those around you that boost your success. Get involved. Get in the spotlight, and don't be afraid to make a fool of yourself. God has you in a life jacket that will keep you afloat when you think you're sinking. You will not fail, because only those who failed fail

Thought of the Day

In our darkest moments, God reveals the way.

The greatest manifestation of the true nature of who we are shows up when we're backed into a corner and are led to our greatest accomplishment.

I would not have been an author if I hadn't gone through some dark moments when I just didn't have enough—moments when I juggled paying bills based on their importance and moments when I had to take days off from work because I couldn't afford gas. Days when I used sick days to catch up with my paycheck at the end of the week.

In those moments, I did my best writing. Those were the moments that pushed me to get published. Those were the moments that turned me into a published author.

Thought of the Day

Our past is a treasure house for our future.

The secret of our future lies in understanding and capitalizing on the things of the past.

Bumps and bruises on the road are a treasure house of triumphs, defeats, and overcoming. They give us opportunities to look back at the things that brought us to our present state. They contain teachable moments that others can use. They contain stories of hope that motivate others. They contain fantasy stories that grab the curiosity of others. Our past has it all. Our past is like one big trophy.

We can treasure our past and use it to capitalize on our future. It becomes the root of our tree, which though unseen, influences the strength of our branches and determines the kind of fruit we will bear.

Thought of the Day

If you plant a few seeds, you'll reap a garden because we reap more than what we sow.

We reap the consequences of our actions, and the consequences tend to outweigh and outlast the actions committed. This encourages us to be careful and thoughtful with our actions.

If we plant anger, we may reap rage, and the effect of rage is greater than the anger planted. Plant fear, we may reap nightmares. Plant peace, and we may reap the silence, restfulness, and stillness of a river. Plant love, and we may reap humanity's embrace of us, lifting us higher. Plant joy, and our hearts may be elevated to a heavenly place of happiness. Plant contentment, and we may receive greater gratitude. Plant generosity, and we may reap showers of praises from those we've changed.

The seeds we plant bring us a greater return, so let's plant with peace, love, and joy in our hearts.

It's okay to laugh over our failures.

I learned at an early age that I should never take life so serious that I was afraid to fail.

I was never a sprinter. I always preferred long-distance running. At fourteen, I almost got lapped in a 100-meter sprint, if that was even possible. Rather than facing the embarrassment of breaking the record for the slowest finish, I pretended to pull a muscle and hopped off the field.

I got sympathy from the spectators—until I explained to them that I faked it. We laughed about it in the end. So I turned my embarrassing failure into laughter.

The late British philosopher Alan Wilson Watts said, "Man suffers only because he takes seriously what the gods made for fun."

15

BELIEF GIVES US ACCESS

Belief is the only requirement for encountering God, and with it miracles can begin.

When I think of belief, I picture a child about to go to sleep in his room. If a parent is in the room, he feels secured and unafraid. If the parent leaves, the child may become scared and even cry. If he doesn't realize the parent left the room, he goes to sleep feeling secured that he is protected by the parent's presence in the room.

When we live with the belief that God is present, we can feel secured and protected as we go about our lives. We can believe in ourselves, believe in others, and believe in God. If we do, we triple our security.

Thought of the Day

Our purpose may scare us, but a good purpose should never deter us.

If survival is all there is to life, life is a useless challenge; survival will always be temporary. So, what can motivate us to live? We can be motivated to find a bigger purpose than the purpose we currently hold. This can be a quest to go deep into the journey to becoming who we are meant to be. It can be a quest to put a positive mark on humanity that will outlive our legacy.

We may not know the people who invented the microwave oven and the cell phone. That's because their achievements outlived their legacies. If our purpose doesn't scare us, it probably isn't big enough. Being scared is not a reason to stop or to change our plan; it can be our motivation to get it done.

You can define your purpose, live in your purpose, and make the world a better place for humanity.

Thought of the Day

If we spend our lives chasing our fears, we will probably die fearful. Instead we can spend our lives chasing our dreams and die fully accomplished with a secure legacy.

I heard a story of a writer who was afraid of flying. He didn't trust anyone to fly him around, and he had no faith in God's protection. So he learned to fly himself, and he flew well. One day, the writer became fearful of the plane he flew, so he learned how to build planes. He built a beautiful plane, and he flew it to many destinations. Then one day a flock of birds flew into his engines, and the plane crashed and burned.

No one remembered him as a pilot or the plane he built. If he had trust in others who can fly him around, and had faith in God's protection, he may have died a writer.

On the couch in his living room, they found the unfinished manuscript of the book he was writing. It was the legacy he was meant to build, but he had forsaken it to chase his fears.

How are we living today? Are we living our dreams, or are we living our fears? Will we trust in God to handle our fears so we can handle our dreams? Remember, our dreams are the things that determine our legacy. By focusing on our dreams, we can make them our reality and leave our survival in God's hands.

Focus on your dreams today, and start living a dream life.

Thought of the Day

A bad script is better than no script at all.

Many times people don't reach their potential because of fear of failure. They keep everything inside them, waiting for the right time to bring it out. The problem is that there is a time limit on anything that's birthing within us, and if we don't bring it out, it dies.

Lloyd Jones, an American athlete who competed in the 800 meter in the 1908 Olympics said that those who try something and fail are infinitely better than those who try nothing and succeed. When we produce something that we dreamed of producing, we become better at producing future products.

Do you have a dream that's growing within you? Go for it, do the work, and bring it to life. We can be producers or consumers. Every dream we bring to life makes us producers. We can dream big and produce in abundance.

Thought of the Day

There was a man who couldn't speak. One day he opened his mouth and made an inaudible sound. The people who knew him well rejoiced and threw a party in his name. One day a stranger heard his voice, and not knowing the man's condition, he shouted, "What an awful voice you have!" From that day on, the man never spoke. Who should we blame for his silence?

The moral of the story is that our voice will not be beautiful for everyone, but it will be beautiful for those who love us the most. In the end, our voice has to be beautiful to us. We shouldn't blame others for our failure to live to our full potential.

Success is defined not only by what we've accomplished, but more importantly by what we've overcome.

Thought of the Day

God has a team already in place for us as we work on accomplishing our goals. We can remain focused and work with our team.

Not everyone will partake in your vision. Be patient. The right team will eventually align with you.

Don't take anyone for granted, because everyone is in your life for a reason and can potentially make your dream a reality.

Keep moving along until you find the right teammates. Remember, not everyone is ready for the journey. Some may be willing but weak. Be patient, and keep building.

Life is a game of can-do, so if we can't do, we can learn from those who can do, until we can do. If we keep company only with those who can't do, nothing will be done. Can't do should never be a permanent state but a call to action.

Thought of the Day

Our thoughts are like pearls in oysters. Not all thoughts produce the perfect pearl, but if we gather them all, we can choose the ones that serve us the most and discard the ones that don't. Then, somewhere along the line, we may create the perfect necklace.

Sometimes we get stuck with the wrong thoughts—those that show us in defeat mode. Then we miss the thoughts that show us the road to success. We walk along the path of failure as it pulls us deeper and deeper into its grasp as things fall apart around us.

We can change things by analyzing the thoughts we focus on, the thoughts that drive our actions. We can focus on thoughts that show us a path to success and act diligently to make them a reality. We can embrace the thoughts that are like pearls in our oysters and build on them until we achieve the perfect necklace.

Just for today, commit to turning things around.

Thought of the Day

We can change the world one light at a time.

What if every act of kindness switched on a light bulb? What if every act of unkindness switched one off? How many lights would we be credited for switching on?

What if we got a chance to review our lights? Would we be staring in amazement at the lights we'd turned on or would we be staring into darkness?

What if we're made to walk in the lights we created? Will we walk in the light? Or will we stumble in the dark?

What if we start turning on the lights in the darkness of our lives?

What if we start with a smile or an act of compassion? We may change the world one light at a time.

Just for today, promise to smile at every situation life presents.

Thought of the Day

Know the strengths of your children, and raise them according to the strengths and interests that they reveal.

Some of us are guilty of raising our kids like bananas when they're actually oranges. They grow up confused and lost, and we wonder where we dropped the ball. God knows what's best for our kids, and he reveals it in their birthright.

We can be vigilant to guide our kids in the areas that they show interest and help turn those interests into opportunities for their growth and development.

Thought of the Day

Even in our sleep, God showers us with mighty gifts. What we do with them when we awake depends on what actions we take. Be vigilant, listen, and act.

I've woken up on many occasions with a song that I don't believe I've previously heard blasting in my head. I'm singing away, and there is an audience. Sometimes I'm not the one singing; sometimes it is someone famous, but the song is mine.

What do I do when I wake up from such an intense revelation? I record what I heard. I try to pen some words to the song. I do research to see if the song already exists and is currently on the radio. If it's a song that's not in existence, I try to get the right team of musicians and singers to bring it into production. Through this method, my song "The Sweetest Love," performed by Sheryl Joseph, got produced.

God sometimes reveals our greatest gifts while we are asleep. Be vigilant, listen, and act.

Thought of the Day

Our greatest transformation comes from those who aren't afraid to push us beyond our comfort zone.

One morning I was jogging on a treadmill at speed four, and I thought I was doing something great. I had my headphones on, with my rap workout music playing and lyrics that I won't repeat.

My beautiful wife and fitness trainer came up beside me and pushed the level up to seven and then up to nine. I was kicked out of my comfort zone and thrown into a real workout. Next she had me do pushups, bench press, and jumps. After the thirty-minute workout and a bottle of water, I was transformed.

Are you being pushed beyond your comfort level, or are you basking in complacency? Sometimes we need others to push us so we can get to the next level. Be open to those who may push you beyond your comfort zone. That may be the catalyst needed for your success.

Thought of the Day

The push is probably the most interesting concept of success.

A car sits in our garage or driveway until we prepare the environment for it to move by getting into it, turning the ignition key, putting it in gear, and putting our foot on the gas pedal. Those pushes move it from stagnation into action.

At camp, my ten-year-old daughter told me she wanted to win a gold medal, but she didn't want to push for it. She wanted to do something really simple to get it. She wanted to get up on a table and dance briefly for everyone. She said she didn't want to risk failure, and she didn't want to make a fool of herself.

I reminded her of the day in the labor room when her mom pushed to get her out of the mess she was in and then welcomed her into the world. I told her that same push mentality is what was going to win her that gold medal—and many more. Success comes with risks and making fools of ourselves. It's the only way to grow and get out of the mess that occurs in stagnation.

I asked her, "Aren't you happy you're still not stuck in Mom's tummy?"

She said, "I get the picture, Dad."

"Now go out there and push yourself. Don't be afraid of failure, and don't be afraid to look foolish. I'll be pushing with you."

Will you help someone push his or her way through to success today?

Thought of the Day

Our best will never be the best for everyone, but it is still our best. We can always strive to be at our best.

Many people in leadership positions have to make decisions that put them at odds with the people they lead. It requires doing what is best for all involved and the risk of not being liked. A strong leader makes the best decision, even if it's unpopular and diminishes his or her likability.

You shouldn't be afraid to make unpopular decisions if they are the best decisions according your understanding. Be at your best, and give your best in all that you do.

Thought of the Day

Success doesn't necessarily emerge for those who sprint, but for those who endure the distance.

There are many moments during the crawls of life when people despair and lose focus. Those who endure crawl before they walk, walk before they run, and eventually are victorious.

Take baby steps. Grow. Then soar. Stay in the race that was meant for you, and success is likely to follow.

Thought of the Day

Somewhere in our muddled past is the future we neglected.

What if we knew our full potential but did everything possible to avoid it? All it may amount to is the creation of a muddled past. What if we took the time to follow the path that we were meant to follow? We can be the best we can be only by being what we were meant to be.

Albert Einstein said that everybody is a genius, but if you judge a fish by its ability to climb a tree, it will live its whole life believing it's stupid.

We can identify our calling in life and live it to our full potential.

Thought of the Day

Clarity of purpose backed by action is the recipe for success.

Have you identified your purpose? This is probably the most important question we can each ask ourselves.

Are we shaping our purpose, or is the world shaping it for us? Have we accomplished our goals? Do we know what our goals are? Have we written our goals down? These questions may sound like those of a nagging spouse, but the answers may provide us with the oil that fuels our drive to be successful and may help us succeed at what we do best.

If we don't know where we're going, can we really get there?

Life, in its simplicity of sleeping, waking, and repeating itself, can be brutal on the lost and discouraged. However, life can be an exciting journey for those who know where they want to go and are working their way there bit by bit, brick by brick, and moment by moment.

When we look at our past, we see either the foundation we've built for the future we so desire or the foundation the world built for us in our quest to survive. One is a permanent foundation; the other is temporary. Jobs come and go, but the decisions and sacrifices we endure to reach our ultimate goal become the foundation of the legacy we aim to build.

Here is a simple assignment to bring clarity into your life journey: Write down your purpose. Write down the steps you are going to take to fulfill that purpose. Write down the things in your past that you've done to build the foundation of the purpose you're building. Then stick to the plan.

Thought of the Day

If we don't find our purpose in life, life will find us a purpose, though it may not be the purpose we were looking for.

To succeed in life, our focus should not be on what it takes to live but on what it takes to win. Success comes to those who intend to win in life. It comes to those who can see the end result of the journey and focus on making it happen.

We shouldn't let life find our purpose for us. We can design our journey today and work toward the finish line, and success will be there waiting to celebrate us.

Create the vision for your purpose, and stick with it till the end.

Thought of the Day

Our wealth will always be where our heart is.

So many times we discard the yearnings of our heart in the pursuit of others who have found success in pursuing their passion. Success does not come to copycats. Success is about finding our own gifts and committing to those gifts one day at a time, brick by brick.

Success may not show us the whole, but it will get us there if we are committed enough.

We can follow our dreams; however humble they may seem. We may not master everything in life; that's not our purpose. But whatever we master, let it serve others and us for the good of humanity.

Trust in God as you go. Let God be the multiplier of your success.

Thought of the Day

Strategic actions and focus open the door to success even in the midst of failure, despair, and hopelessness.

What do we do when we face challenges? Do we attack them aimlessly? Do we come up with a plan of action? Do we stick to the plan, or do we give in to distractions? Do we look at the actions taken by those who overcome challenges like the ones we face? Do we take the time to reassess our strengths, talents, and goals with a focus on bettering ourselves?

Life challenges us to attain our freedom by becoming the most authentic version of ourselves. It challenges us to maintain focus and be committed and vigilant in safeguarding and developing the things that are important to us. Whether it is love, peace of mind, or success, the principles are all the same.

Avoid distractions; stay focus; develop skills; learn from others; and create an environment of love, peace, and success. Even in the deepest tragedies, success can rise if we remain strategic and focused, and reach to attain our goals.

If our goal is love, we can be committed to and focus on love. If our goal is peace, we can be committed to and create and surround ourselves with an environment that supports peace. We can be committed and reinvent ourselves so that we are focused and strategic in staying on the path that leads to our success.

Remember, anything that isn't part of your plan is a distraction. Weed out distractions and stay focused, and success will come in ways you've never imagined possible. Through it all, have faith in God. He will see you through.

Thought of the Day

When we settle our dreams on volcanoes, we shouldn't be alarmed by eruptions. We must keep moving.

Life has a way of making us uncomfortable when we're not in the right place. We hear the rumblings, but we treat it as just another day. Some of us dig in and settle on our rumbles. We drink, smoke, worry, spend recklessly, ignore our spirituality. We make the rumbles our home. We assume they're going to go away. Then they erupt into a full-scale volcano and send us in a tailspin.

We can adopt an ear for rumblings and use it to reassess our situation. A rumbling may be temporary, but if it's been happening for a long time, it may be telling us it's time to get moving; it's time to make changes. It can be the motivation we need to aim for bigger and greater things.

Just for today, let your rumbles be the motivation that spring you into action and move you away from the volcanoes of life.

Thought of the Day

Every new day is a second-chance day. We just have to see it that way.

What would you do if your slate was wiped clean and you were given a fresh start? What would you do different if yesterday's troubles were mysteriously erased? Would you look for new troubles to replace the old, or would you live a trouble-free life?

Every new day is a chance to make amends for the wrong turns we've made. It is a chance to get things right. It is a chance to live our best life. It is a chance for us to succeed in areas where we once failed. Make today count. Go out and be successful.

Thought of the Day

Go forth quietly and persistently along the path of life that is made for you.

Are you living your dream? Do you wake up each day with an eagerness to fulfill your dream? Or are you living to pay the bills? Do you have the satisfaction you want out of life? Would you rather be doing something different?

These are important questions you must ask yourself if you are to understand the path you're on. The ideal path will be the one that leads you along the roads of your dreams. While life does not guarantee your success or failure, the path that's meant for you will guarantee your full satisfaction.

Guatama Buddha said that if you do not change direction, you may end up where you are heading.

We can avoid distractions and stick to the path that was made for us.

No one builds an empire on stagnation.

A stagnant empire is an empire in turmoil. It is one on the brink of defeat.

If God gives you a thought, envision a book. If God gives you a house, envision a hotel. If God gives you a restaurant, envision a franchise. When God gives you a life, envision a legacy.

Success comes when we walk in our greatness, learn from our greatness, and keep growing in our greatness.

Be great in everything you choose to do.

Thought of the Day

Don't carry a leaking bucket list.

You can do the things in life that you are passionate about, whether short term or long term. Otherwise, you'll live in regret at the end of your days.

Life is fast-paced. The only thing that seems to slow life down is when we're having intense fun. Have you ever watched the final minute of a close basketball game? The intensity of the event seems to slow life down.

The career plans that cause us momentary excitement may be the ones that need to be on our bucket list. Sometimes we jump into action immediately, but then we retreat and start talking ourselves out of our plans. Negativity starts to speak to our wounds, and we retreat to the back of the line.

Success is never retreat. Success pushes along to the finish line, never looking back, always looking ahead.

Success is like climbing a ladder to the top of Mount Everest. We may take stops along the way, but retreating is not an option. We keep pushing on with our journey until we reach the pinnacle of success.

Thought of the Day

When we find our purpose, we find our joy.

Many of us have ignored our purpose. We've judged our gifts and abandoned them along the way.

God has a purpose for each of us, and I believe that purpose was instilled in us from birth. We can pay close attention to ourselves and our children to discover our gifts.

Doors you're attached to close unexpectedly through no fault of your own. Have no fear. Don't go into panic mode. It can be God's way of steering you back on track to where you truly belong. Use the opportunity to pursue your purpose.

Thought of the Day

Success has a high price tag, but if all you see is the price, you may miss your opportunity to succeed.

Invest in success. Be sure that the heat in your kitchen is energizing you and not turning you into toast. Pursue the goals and dreams that were meant for you, not those that were meant for others. You can't fail at doing you, but you sure can at doing others.

The late Indian business tycoon Dhirubhai Ambani, who founded Reliance Industries in Bombay, said that if you don't build your dreams, someone else will hire you to build theirs.

Whose dream are you building? Is it your own, or is it someone else's? Commit to your dreams, and success will likely follow.

Thought of the Day

The people closest to us can talk us out of our dreams to protect themselves and us.

Think about it. David would have never become king if he had told his dad he was going to fight Goliath with three pebbles and a slingshot. Not even his brothers knew until they saw Goliath fall.

Our biggest dreams may seem impossible to everyone except us. We have to be killing lions in our private time so that when we meet our Goliath, it will be a walk in the park.

If your friend next door finds success with his dream, that doesn't mean you can find success following *his* dream. Remember, your biggest dream is going to look and sound ridiculous to those closest to you, but you can stay focused and reach for it anyway.

Thought of the Day

Great success is an underdog story. The greater the odds against us, the greater our success will be.

Many of us panic when things go wrong. We run away from the situation. We give up on the struggles. We surrender without a fight. We destroy our joy. We adopt a loser mentality.

What we fail to realize is that the deeper our pitfalls in life, the sweeter and greater our victory. It means we can refocus on what we do best and bring it to the forefront of what we are. It is a chance for us to step up and play our strongest game.

Just for today, we can focus on our A game. We can bring out the best in everything we do. Everyone will watch us ascend. Everyone likes a great victory. Everyone cheers for the underdogs. Let's play our best game today.

The sweetest hay we'll ever make is the hay we make from where we lay.

Ours is a fast-paced life, and time is limited. Sometimes we're up and sometimes we're down. The down time is a good signal for us to change gear, speed up, and get moving. Yes, it's okay to throw a pity party when we're down, but all parties must come to an end. Soon the guests leave, and we may find that we're the only ones left at our party.

Don't despair. Get back in the race. Run harder and faster. When God is on your side, failure will be a part of your past. The best victories are those snatched from the jaws of defeat.

Believe in yourself. Trust in God. Persevere, and snatch your victory.

Thought of the Day

Discomfort is how we grow, and to experience growth we have to move with urgency.

A frail old man in a wheelchair went down to the river to meet a wise sage for healing. As the old man approached, the sage kicked the wheelchair from under him. The old man scrambled on the ground and crawled back into the chair. He was startled and visibly upset.

As he climbed into his chair, the wise sage grabbed him by the neck, tossed him into the river, and held his head underwater. The old man gasped, kicked, and screamed. Just before he gasped his last breath, the wise man lifted him out of the water and tossed him back onto the land.

The old man was in a rage and ran to find the nearest boulder. He lifted it and aimed it at the sage. Just as he was about to land his fatal blow, the sage stopped him and asked, "Didn't you come to see me in a wheelchair, and are you not now standing? Do you show your gratitude by throwing stones at the one who healed you?"

Disgruntledly, the old man climbed back into his wheelchair and rode away.

Could that be you? Have you ever prayed for something and when God gave it to you, you either didn't recognize it or you complained or fought against it? How do you treat your finances? How do you treat your spouse? How do you treat your health?

Sometimes shock therapy is the only way to lift us out of our bondage of self-pity and fearfulness, and bring us back to a life of gratitude and good health.

Thought of the Day

We spend a lifetime trying to know ourselves, while the world spends a lifetime trying to mold us into who it wants us to be.

Who are you? Are you a husband or a wife? Are you a parent? Or are you a child? These questions can be answered with clarity.

Unfortunately, questions keep on coming, and the answers become less clear.

What is your purpose? Do you know what motivates you? What makes you smile? What gives you the will to wake up and look forward to life? Are you living life to the fullest?

Who is your Creator? Do you have a relationship with your Creator? Do you spend time in the presence of your Creator? Have you abandoned your Creator, and are you feeling the effects of that abandonment?

Regardless of the questions we have about unclear areas of our lives, we can find answers when we pray and listen in silence without interrupting our thoughts. The answers will come, and when they do, we'll be able to answer all the questions as easily as we say I am a husband; I am a wife; I am parent; I am a child; I know my purpose; I know my God.

Thought of the Day

No one walks into a barbershop and demands the old hair back. So why do we treat the new day like the old?

Do you ever wake up in the morning and sink back into the previous day before you get a chance to embrace the new day? Even before we get a chance to look outside to see what the new day has delivered, we sometimes embrace yesterday's sorrows, yesterday's fear, and yesterday's hurt. It's almost like we're demanding our old haircut before we get a chance to try the new.

But we don't have to succumb to the temptation of falling back into old ways. When our thoughts start retracting into the old, we can put our hands up and shout praises for the new day. We can shout, "The devil is a liar!" We can take a look in the mirror and admire our haircut. We can give thanks to the barber for a job well done.

Who is giving you your nightly cuts? Who is the one that's renewing your faith and your strength to pursue life? Do you know which one is the lie and which one is the truth?

Embrace joy and happiness regardless of your circumstances. Treat each day like a new haircut.

16

UNITY IS MORE THAN STRENGTH

Thought of the Day

We will win the war of race when the message is changed from my race and your race to our race. We will win the war on religion when the message is changed from my religion and your religion to our religion.

When we approach our problems from the position of our problems, we can grow from strength to strength together as we seek workable solutions. We are destroyed not by our strength in unity but by the chaos and noise of our weakest links.

When we take responsibility for the state of our world, it opens the door for us to start making a difference.

Thought of the Day

Before we respond to a criticism, we can ask for a solution.

Critiques block solutions to problems. Before we criticize people, we should tell them our solutions. And before we criticize someone for criticizing us, we should ask him or her for a solution.

At a recent book sale event, my ten-year-old daughter criticized me for the slow book sales. We had spent an hour there and had sold only three books. I told her it seemed I was doing all the work as she played on my phone. I reminded her that I was paying her for the event, and if she didn't participate, she would lose out on future opportunities to get paid. My ego was getting the better of me.

But then I did something different. I told her that I welcomed her criticism and asked her what she would do differently to boost sales. We had a big board promoting the event, and she got up, grabbed a couple of markers, and started writing a few things that were missing. She wrote the cost of the book and underlined it with a red line. She wrote that the candies were free, and she wrote that the number of books was limited.

I was too busy nursing my ego to look at what she had written. Then it happened. People coming in looked at the board and then came to the table to purchase books. Then I looked at the board myself and saw that the price of the book stood out boldly. That was the missing link to our success.

I'm glad I asked for a solution before I let my ego block her criticisms.

Thought of the Day

We can rise above the level of the previous day's happiness.

We can get excited about something new or about an improvement on something we did the previous day. There is still a wealth of opportunities within our scope and waiting to be discovered. But if we can't find an opportunity, there is never a shortage of love to give.

We can treat life like a cruise and see ourselves as the passengers. God has provided for us, and we can provide for others. We also can create opportunities for others to provide for themselves.

Thought of the Day

God may bless us and guide us to green pastures if we stop interrupting him.

So many times God opens new doors and blessings, but we bring back old habits that have been disruptive and walk right out of the green pastures that he has led us into. We disrupt the harmony of the experience to go back to our old ways, and we miss our opportunity for greatness. Then we complain to a patient God that things aren't going that well and that we need his help. It's almost like winning the lottery and squandering our winnings.

We pray to get married, fall in love, get married, and then fall right out of love. We pray for the dream job, get hired, and then find a way to get fired. We find many ways to sabotage God's blessings. We find ways to sabotage our success.

It doesn't have to be this way. We can stay committed to the things that are important and do what it takes to turn things around.

Speak your truth. Stay focus. Be patient. Be persistent. Be polite. Be kind. Carry love in your heart, even when the potential for anger burns. Seek understanding. Change will come.

Just for today, trust in God's blessings over your life and treat your life like a blessing.

Thought of the Day

In this complex matrix called life, for every one that leads there are multiple followers, and yet everyone that follows is a leader.

Want to make a difference? Find your relevance and stick to it. We can't be everything for everyone, but we can be true to ourselves. Our relevance is as unique to us as fruit is to the tree that bears it. An orange tree doesn't bear mangoes, and a mango tree doesn't try to bear oranges. We can make the difference only in the areas of our strengths.

We can accomplish more when we allow others to work in areas that complement their strengths and make up for their weaknesses. This is a good strategy for building the perfect team.

Thought of the Day

Our success is built on the sacrifice of others, whether we like to admit it or not.

A mother sacrifices for her child. Parents sacrifice for their family. Workers sacrifice for their employer. Employers sacrifice for their employees. Customers sacrifice for businesses. Congregants sacrifice for their church. Pastors sacrifice for their congregation. The list can go on and on.

When we say that we did it alone, we are being selfish. We become victims of our own misunderstandings. Be humble with success. Express gratitude. Show appreciation to those who sacrificed to make success possible.

Thought of the Day

We may never rise to our true potential until we get over our dependencies.

Like a boat stranded on the ocean, we are all souls in transit. You would do well to ask yourself, "What can I do to make the transition better for me and for others?" Then act on it in whatever way you can. Small or big, it doesn't matter. Just act.

Each of us can make a difference, and when it's over, may death greet us with a smile on our face and no fear in our heart. May death greet us with peace and not anger. May death greet us with love and not malice; compassion and not resistance; humility and not greed; joy and not sadness; contentment for a job well done and not regret.

May we move from a position of dependency to where we can be depended on.

Thought of the Day

It's important to have enemies because friends don't have all the answers.

Like-minded people lead each other on the same path, and if that path becomes stagnant and destructive, like-minded people perish in harmony.

Those we perceive as enemies may lead us onto dangerous paths. The challenge we face is discernment—the ability to know what is right and what is wrong. If we follow blindly, we must take responsibility for our own destruction.

Nothing opens up the path to knowledge and growth better than those who see things differently than we do.

Follow others, but don't follow blindly. Ask questions. Seek clarifications. Look at things from all sides. Learn with diligence.

Thought of the Day

We complete each other near and far, weak and strong, successful and unsuccessful. In our completeness, we create the perfect world, where love, peace, and success abide in harmony.

Have you wondered what would happen if a tired nose decided it was doing all the breathing and demanded that the mouth take over the breathing. What if the mouth demanded that a hand take over? What if the hand agreed? If it did, life would cease.

What if the hand got tired of feeding the mouth? Sure the mouth can feed itself, but a mouth needs a hand for things beyond its reach.

As a writer, I sometimes wish I were a great speaker. As a songwriter, I wish I could play an instrument or could hold a note and not have it disintegrate into an annoying pitch. Fortunately, I've had speakers, singers, and musicians who complete me better than I complete myself.

I try not to miss the opportunity to network with those who possess the key to my completeness, even while I'm aware that I too possess the key to their completeness.

Today is a good day to come alongside someone who is in need of completeness and is determined to work hard to make it a reality.

Thought of the Day

Like them or not, opinions help us grow. But what good is an opinion if it is kept to itself? An opinion expressed is better than an opinion suppressed.

Before you address an opinion, seek clarity from the one that stated it. This can lead to understanding and friendship. It can also lead to growth.

We all have views on many issues. When we lose patience with each other and block each other, we no longer progress. We may not agree on everything, and that's okay, but dialogue is a step toward progress.

The eighteenth-century German scientist Georg Christop Lichtenberg said, "One must judge men not by their opinions, but by what their opinions have made of them."

Thought of the Day

Multitasking with *nots* can be the silent killer of the untrained mind.

Many of us are heavily burdened by oppressive thoughts. We allow our thoughts to rob our peace of mind. Even as we go about with joy in our hearts, there is a wall of pain that reminds us we shouldn't be joyful, for hurt can be just around the corner. We are so consumed by potential hurt that we walk right into it with open arms. We make poor decisions about the things that provide for our security: our spirituality, our finances, our relationships, our health, our commitments. We willfully surrender it all because we've bought into the idea that hurt and failure are imminent.

What if we increased our fight? What if we challenged the impossible? What if we strived to accomplish the things that we deem impossible? If we did, we would find it easier to do the things that are possible.

What if, when someone whispers that we won't amount to anything, we used it as a motivation to achieve our goals? What if when someone says we'll never be wealthy, we use it as a motivation to build our wealth?

I attended a prophecy class at our local church in which the pastor decided we should have a group laugh about the negative things people say about us. One woman started it by saying, "They said I wouldn't amount to anything." Loud laughter broke out in the room. Another woman said, "They said I would never beat this cancer." Laughter broke out again. I was a little hesitant at first, but the woman who said it was laughing, so I decided it wouldn't hurt to laugh. I had a good laugh. Another shouted, "They said that God doesn't answer prayers." This time I had no problem laughing.

At the end of the exercise, the entire room was happy. The weight was off our shoulders, and we had a strong bond of love for each other.

Thought of the Day

In the midst of our storms, we can shout our victories because our circumstances do not define us.

Many of us go through storms, but when we become consumed with the storms, we forget how great we are. We forget the great storms we've battled and overcome. We see the despair and not the hope. What if we refuse to accept defeat in the midst of our storms? What if we give it the fight of our lives? What if we speak only words of victory over our storms? What if we gather our best team of storm killers?

In the midst of our storms, we can cast our nets of hope, our nets of peace, our nets of love, our nets of victory.

We can go wherever the storm may lead us, but with victory in our hearts, minds, and souls. And remember that somewhere beyond our horizon, victory awaits us. Keep the hope alive.

About the Author

Ricardo Williams was born in Grenada, West Indies. This is his second published book. His first book was *"Dear God, An Impatient Conversation with A Patient God."* It was a personal testimony in his quest to grasp a deeper meaning of his relationship with Christ.

He started off his writing career as a songwriter. He wrote the song, *"The Sweetest Love,"* performed by Sheryl Joseph in 2009. The song was played on Caribbean radio stations.

He became a comedy writer in 1996 for the Heritage Theater Group in Grenada and did some standup comedy. He toured with the group to perform in a play at the International Theater Festival in Aruba in 1996.

He started blogging in 2005 and had over 100,000 in viewership.

He won a pair of airline seats from American Airlines after winning a writing contest they sponsored in 2002. Ricardo Williams has a Bachelor of Science in Business Management from Devry University. He was president of Chrysler Financial Toastmasters for two terms. He wrote articles for Circle T, a corporate magazine publication for Mercedes Benz Financial. He lives in Cedar Hill, Texas, and is married to Anjanette Williams. They have a daughter Zuri Williams, and two sons, Amir, and Kelayda.

Printed in the United States
By Bookmasters